THE GILDED CAGE

Lesley Oliver

"The real deal ... It is a must read, a guide and a recovery book for anyone contemplating leaving an abusive relationship. Lesley addresses dealing with fear, doubt, and self-esteem and shows how her inner strength took her from despair to wholeness and completion."

Di Riddell
Author of *Beyond Abuse – a recovery guide for men and women in an era of me and all of us too*
Speaker and Confidence Coach

"Heroism is not in flying cape grand gestures but in the daily endurance of the unendurable and holding onto self-worth amidst unrelenting degradation. Real and inspiring ... The Gilded Cage will help women everywhere to speak up and to rescue themselves."

Irene Green
Co-owner of Harcourts International Ltd. 9 countries.
Founder of Inspirational Women.
Operating across Australia, New Zealand, South Africa and USA, Inspirational Women is a program that encourages women to step to the podium to share their true stories to help others.

"I found it captivating – it held my attention so much so that I read it in one sitting. Each chapter lured you to the next chapter as you followed her story and watched a strong amazing resilient and compassionate person unfold. This book is an easy read and speaks to you. I commend this book to all those who are seeking a guiding light to break free from their situation."

Trish Springsteen
Australia's Leading Expert in Empowering Introverts
Multi International Award-Winning Mentor, Speaker
International Best-Selling Author – 14 books
www.trishspringsteen.com

THE GILDED CAGE

I broke free
 from the gilded cage of
  White Collar Domestic Violence
            … and you can, too.

The Gilded Cage

Copyright © 2019 Lesley Oliver

First published 2019

Published by MJL Publications

17 Spencer Avenue
　Deception Bay QLD 4508
　Australia

Edited by Snowflake Productions

Cover image by Thomas Oliver

This book is an account of my experience of 'white collar' domestic violence, told to the best of my ability and recollection. Names have been changed to protect the privacy of certain individuals.

All rights reserved. Without limiting the right under Copyright reserved above, no part of this publication may be reproduced, stored in or introduced into a database and retrieval system, or transmitted in any form or by any means (electronic, mechanical, photocopying, recording or otherwise) without the prior written permission of owner of the Copyright on the above author and publishers.

*I dedicate this book to my remarkable son,
for his faith, courage and resilience.
He continues to inspire me.*

*To my mother, whose love and support
made leaving the Gilded Cage possible.*

To the friends who helped me in my darkest hours.

*And to anyone experiencing domestic violence –
know that there is always hope.*

Foreword

This book is a must-read for anyone interested in learning more about Domestic Family Violence (DFV). Lesley Oliver takes us on a journey of how she blindly and unknowingly lived in an abusive relationship for 14 years before realizing that she was raising her son in a toxic marriage.

The Gilded Cage is a factual account of her marriage in which she felt trapped and unable to escape. She has shared her story in three parts including her life, her plan to escape and finally she discusses how she navigated the long journey of separation and the Family Court system in Australia.

Lesley shares with us the non-physical aspects of the DFV she endured, giving an actual insight into the life of a seemingly affluent marriage but revealing the horrific day to day torment and control within the confines of their home.

Having a detailed safety plan too often can mean the difference between living below the poverty line or being able to feed your children. Lesley describes the process she went through, cleverly identifying the safety steps she put in place as she planned her escape from an abusive marriage.

Lastly, Lesley gives invaluable insight and information for others to glean from to know what to do after you have left, and in particular how having an effective and water tight safety plan in place can help you navigate the legal system in Australia.

The page turner kept me intrigued and in my opinion is a valuable resource for anyone who might be experiencing DFV or has a family member, friend or neighbour who is experiencing DFV, so they have an idea of how to identify and then help. As the CEO of a not-for-profit (NFP) charity that provides support to families affected by DFV, I highly recommend this book as a tool for those wanting to know more.

Karen Johns B.Ed.; B.Min.
CEO/Founder DARE Formal Wear Ltd
(Domestic Abuse Recovery and Education)

Table of Contents

INTRODUCTION 1
PART ONE 9
ONE | In the beginning 11
TWO | A fine romance... 23
THREE | Into the gilded cage 33
FOUR | A 'charmed' life... 41
FIVE | The winds of change 57
SIX | Moving the goalposts 69
SEVEN | Detachment 77
EIGHT | Serendipity 93
PART TWO.. 101
NINE | ...and your enemies closer......................... 103
TEN | The battle plan 115
ELEVEN | The final countdown.............................. 127
TWELVE | Exodus 135
THIRTEEN | A new order.. 145
FOURTEEN | Back to business 159
FIFTEEN | Opportunity knocks.............................. 167
PART THREE 177
SIXTEEN | Survival of the organised 179
SEVENTEEN | So, how do I do this?...................... 193

EIGHTEEN | Judgement day 211
NINETEEN | The final act 221
TWENTY | Lessons learned 227
Acknowledgements 231

INTRODUCTION

I am strong because I've been weak

I am fearless because I've been afraid

I am wise because I've been foolish

I'm not a victim seeking sympathy, nor am I an authority on the issue of domestic violence. I am, however, someone who lived through years of it and I share my story with you so you may know how invisible domestic and family violence in its various forms can be, how difficult it can be to understand, and how easy it is to slip under its silent control. This can happen to you, your sister, your daughter, or your friend – domestic violence does not discriminate.

I have written the book in three parts. Part one explores different types of domestic violence, and what it is like to live under its gossamer-like veil. Part two describes my military-like covert operation to escape to a new life. And part three follows my journey to seek justice via self-representation in the Australian Family Court system.

THE GILDED CAGE

We most often associate the term domestic violence with physical abuse, and this is understandable as it is the most graphic and obvious form of it. But domestic violence can be subtle, sophisticated, and imperceptible to the uninitiated. It takes many guises and too often we forget that physical abuse is but one of its manifestations. Emotional abuse, financial abuse, sexual abuse, social abuse and verbal abuse are other types of domestic violence; no less destructive but infinitely easier to conceal. It's what I think of as 'white collar' abuse – it leaves no physical mark on the victim – but it is absolute in its ability to control them, to paralyse them with fear. Let's be clear about one thing, whatever form it takes, domestic violence is a violation of human rights. It is not acceptable, it is not excusable, and it is certainly not part of a normal healthy relationship.

If you don't think that family violence is a problem, the facts may convince you otherwise. The statistics below are from Australian sources; however, the prevalence of domestic violence is fairly consistent across the developed world.

- One in three women have experienced physical and/or sexual violence perpetrated by someone known to them [1]

INTRODUCTION

- Domestic and family violence is the principal cause of homelessness for women and their children [2]
- Over 12 months, on average, one woman is killed every week by a current or former partner [3]
- A woman killed by her partner is most likely to be killed in her home [4]
- 2 in 5 assaults reported to police in 2016 were family- or domestic violence-related [5]
- Indigenous women and girls are 35 times more likely than the wider female population to be hospitalised due to family violence [6]

Controlling behaviours develop gradually over time so that the victim may not recognise that they are in an abusive relationship. This may seem ludicrous to an observer but consider that the perpetrator has been progressively and expertly stripping away their victim's sense of self-worth by stealth. Seemingly benign comments about a person's appearance, or their intelligence, unfavourable comparisons with other people, influencing their choice of clothes and so on, can be just the beginning of a well-orchestrated campaign to immobilise their target.

THE GILDED CAGE

Drip, drip, drip. Daily criticisms can erode your sense of self-worth as completely as any beating. A simple drop of water seems harmless enough, certainly nothing that could damage anything as robust as stone. And yet it is the constant dripping of little drops of water over time that erodes great chunks of rock.

> *"Water dripping day by day, wears the hardest rock away".*
> Portuguese proverb.

Intimidation, financial control, withholding affection, jealousy and possessiveness – often used in unison – are just some of the weapons in the abuser's extensive arsenal. When denial fuels the abuse and the cycle of violence becomes the norm, it seems that there is no solution and no safe way out. Yet it doesn't have to be this way.

It is all too easy to demonise the perpetrator. Why do they do what they do? It's a very good question and it doesn't have a simple one-size-fits-all answer. I can only speak from my own experience and suggest that it's a complex mix of factors, a perfect storm of stimuli. Gender norms and inequality can play a part, as can cultural influences. Desensitisation through exposure to violence can be a potent driver, and alcohol and

INTRODUCTION

substance abuse relax otherwise effective self-controls. Violent and abusive behaviours are learnt, and they are used intentionally to exercise power and control.

Do the abusers need help? Absolutely. How we help them is not the focus of this book, but nor do I wish to dismiss the issue. While it might seem absurd, I believe that the perpetrators of domestic violence are victims too. Acknowledging that they are abusive, controlling or violent is the first step towards them seeking help to break the cycle. There are any number of recognised services that help perpetrators to overcome their violent and controlling behaviours. But it first requires them to admit that they have a problem and then to accept help, for any program to be effective.

The truth is most men don't abuse women and most men don't think that violence against women is acceptable. While domestic violence is most likely to be perpetrated by a man against a woman, I acknowledge that men are often the forgotten victims of domestic violence. So, let us not forget that female domestic violence against men exists and that domestic violence also occurs in Lesbian, Gay, Bisexual, Transgender, Intersex and Queer (LGBTIQ) relationships too.

THE GILDED CAGE

I have written this book to lift the veil on how insidious and sophisticated domestic and family violence can be, to show you how to recognise it, to help you break free from it under your own terms, and to guide you so you may successfully navigate your way through the complex maze that is the Australian Family Law system. And while this is a true story, I have elected to change the names of those people represented in this book to protect their privacy and my own.

If my story resonates with you in any way, please seek help before it is too late. Don't wait for things to improve, because it is unlikely that they will; the best indicator of someone's future behaviour is their past behaviour. If you think this book would help someone you know, please pass it on. He or she may not be ready for the message today, but maybe they will be tomorrow.

And finally, my message to you is that there is always hope. You have it within yourself to break free safely, and to take control of your circumstances for the life you deserve. No one can do it for you, but you can do it with the help of others. I did it and you can too. It starts with a leap of faith.

INTRODUCTION

You are stronger than you know

You are bolder than you imagine

You are wiser than you believe

THE GILDED CAGE

Citations:

[1] Australian Bureau of Statistics. (2013), *Personal Safety, Australia, 2012*, cat. No. 4906.0. Retrieved from: http://bit.ly/1kKSe0I © White Ribbon Australia 2014

[2] Australian Institute of Health and Welfare. (2013) Specialist homelessness services 2012-13. cat no. HOU 273. Retrieved from: http://bit.ly.1ofyA7s © White Ribbon Australia 2014

[3] Chan, A. and Payne, J. (2013). Homicide in Australia: 2008-09 to 2009-10, *National Homicide Monitoring Program annual report*. Canberra: Australia: Australian Institute of Criminology. Retrieved from: http://bit.ly/lqVoTZF © White Ribbon Australia

[4] Mitchell. L. (2011), Domestic violence in Australia – an overview of the issues. Canberra, Australia: Department of Parliamentary Services. Retrieved from: http://1.usa.gov/XGoTDZ p.923 © White Ribbon Australia 2014

[5] Data from NSW, SA, WA, Tas, NT and ACT. Assault data not published for VIC and Qld. Australian Bureau of Statistics. (2017). Recorded Crime – Victims, Australia, 2016, cat. No 4510.0. Retrieved from: http://bit.ly/2woZeSG © White Ribbon Australia 2017

[6] Council of Australian Governments, (2010). *National Plan to Reduce Violence Against Women and Their Children 2010 – 2022*. Retrieved from: http://bit.ly/1mowHQu © White Ribbon Australia 2014

Reproduced with kind permission from White Ribbon Australia

PART ONE

ONE | In the beginning

He knows. Oh, dear God, I think he knows! He is standing in the doorway, looking back at me before he leaves for work. I see a look on his face that I have never seen before. I have seen malice, I have seen contempt, and I have seen disgust, but this is new; it is intense, and it burns right through me. My heart is thumping in my chest and yet I am keeping up the pretence, as I am conditioned to do, with a neutral expression on my face. **Nothing going on here.** His stare lasts for what seems like an eternity, then finally he turns and walks out of the door. It is time for me to go too, but I won't be coming back.

A few days earlier…

> It is a Wednesday afternoon in late June 2003 and a woman reports to her local police station in suburban Brisbane to tell somebody, anybody, that she fears for her life. Brisbane winters are mild and yet she shakes uncontrollably. The police officer behind the counter asks her to wait and disappears. The woman stands there awkwardly with her mother by her side, unsure that she will be taken seriously, but with nothing left to lose, she waits patiently…

THE GILDED CAGE

No more than a minute or two passes and she is ushered into a side office by a senior policeman, the senior sergeant in charge of the station. Stepping through the door, there is no turning back. **Click** – the door shuts. **Click, Clack** – the cogs start to turn, setting in motion a series of events that will be life-changing for her and those around her.

That woman is me: fearful, exhausted, resolute. It has taken me 14 years to reach this point; is it courage or hopelessness, or perhaps both, that have brought me there? For the next 15 minutes or so I detail the events that have led to this surreal scene…I sob quietly as I explain the abusive marriage, the controlling behaviours, and the realization that if I didn't get out now, I may never. I have a plan in place to get my son and me out of this mess and I need the police to be aware of where and when it will happen. Just in case things don't go to plan, someone needs to know, and to ask questions.

The police officer listens to me, he asks questions, he is respectful, and he includes my mother in the conversation. She speaks when I cannot. He confirms that what I have described to him is domestic violence. What a bittersweet moment this is – validation and acceptance of something I

ONE | In the beginning

would rather not acknowledge. I am articulate, polite and well presented; middle-class right down to my suede boots. I do not fit the picture I had previously imagined of a victim of domestic violence. Yet at my lowest points I did see myself as a victim: a victim of my own stupidity and trusting nature. Why didn't I question things? Why didn't I demand answers? Because I knew I would not have been given any, and it was dangerous to ask.

I see concern on the sergeant's face when I mention the presence of unregistered firearms in the house. They were not surrendered during the 1996-1997 Australian gun amnesty. A legacy of the terrible Port Arthur tragedy, the firearms buy-back scheme reflected the widespread change in attitude to gun ownership. The government purchased over 600,000 newly-prohibited shotguns and rapid-fire rifles at market value from gun owners, and tens of thousands of other non-prohibited firearms were voluntarily surrendered, with no recompense. But my husband saw himself above the law and kept his weapons nonetheless. A visual reminder of who had absolute control.

THE GILDED CAGE

A note is made of the day and time that I will be leaving the family home – Friday sometime after 6pm – and an assurance given that the police will be in the area.

I will be eternally grateful for the acceptance and concern shown to me at the police station. Domestic violence was only just starting to be recognised and discussed in mainstream society, and I had genuine concerns that I might have been wasting my time speaking to the authorities. If not for the kindness and professionalism of that police officer, what follows may never have happened…

How is it possible that another person can control someone so completely? The clues are there if you look closely and the place to start is at the very beginning. My early life was fairly standard: Dad, Mum and two kids living in a modest home on the semi-rural outskirts of Sydney, Australia. My father was a schoolteacher, a quietly spoken man who enjoyed classical music, the written word and tinkering in his garage. He was kind and gentle and funny, and I adored him with every fibre of my being. My mother was something different altogether. Strong, strict and unyielding, she ruled with an iron will. She was a strict disciplinarian and, in fairness to her, it made life

ONE | In the beginning

simple to know where the boundaries were and exactly what would happen if you stepped outside them.

My brother Euan was five years older than me, and he didn't care about the boundaries or what the consequences would be for crossing them. He was defiant, precociously intelligent and universally unafraid. In fact, it seemed that he enjoyed getting into trouble, and enjoyed the drama that followed even more. Mum wouldn't give an inch, there was no compromising from her, and so the dance between them would begin with Euan transgressing in some way; it really didn't take much to get things started. Firstly, there would be yelling from both sides, followed by the fight back from Euan, and then finally the punishment from Mum. The penalty was usually administered with the cane end of a feather duster, Mum's weapon of choice. Afterwards Euan would shrug things off, as if he didn't care at all, an act of defiance to show Mum that she hadn't really won.

But Euan was more than just a feisty child: he was tall, hilariously funny and smart, and as the eldest of the kids in our neighbourhood (who were mostly boys), he was the natural leader of the group. It was a real treat for me to be included in hanging out with the older kids, especially as I was the youngest, and a *girl!* Most homes had large back gardens then, and there was no shortage of space to play games, so backyard cricket was a given on any summer weekend or during the school holidays. Being the youngest, and a *girl*, I was allowed to join in the cricket games, but mostly as an outfielder, and rarely as a batter, unless there had been a middle-order batting collapse.

I remember one occasion when Euan gave me the go-ahead to bat after our star batsman Skinny Sullivan was struck down with a bout of the 'trots' after trying to prove that you could eat an ice-cream, and a cream bun, and drink a can of soft drink in under 60 seconds. As I stared down the bowler, I think that I should have been technically out on a 'Golden Duck' (for the uninitiated, that's the first ball bowled), but Euan showed leniency to me in consideration of my obvious handicaps, that is being younger and smaller than all the others, and of course being a *girl*. I was allowed to bat on for an extraordinary amount of time with blatant lbw's (leg-before-wicket) being waived by Euan, who pointed out that, as the cricket bat came up to near my armpits, I might struggle to swing it with any accuracy.

ONE | In the beginning

Putting my short-lived cricket triumph aside, I was a naturally shy and quiet child. My earliest memories are of me standing behind my mother with my face in her skirt as she answered the front door. "Oh, take no notice of her, she's just shy," she would say to the caller, to reassure them that it was normal behaviour for me, and no reflection on them.

I loathed the all-too-frequent arguments between Mum and Euan and did everything I could to avoid getting into trouble myself. Now that wasn't easy as Mum had very high standards and imposed strict rules. No talking back – ever, proper manners at all times, no sitting on beds, no bare feet in the house (it took the shine off the polished floor boards), no noise (it jangled her nerves), no toys left about, no asking for anything. We soon learned that if you asked for something it was 'the kiss of death', as it all but guaranteed that you wouldn't get what you wanted. For me it was far preferable to toe the line than to face any punishment. If I got the cane, I would be distraught for days, and fearful of another hiding. In fairness, we weren't the only kids feeling the sharp end of the feather duster: back then it was more common for parents to administer discipline this way. I'm not saying that it was right, but it was considered acceptable by many. Consequently, as a small child I was frightened of my mother and my whole day was spent doing nothing to provoke her. *Keep out of the way, don't do anything to attract attention.* And so, the shy child also became the observant child. *Watch and learn, keep your head down, and stay safe.*

My darling father was not a well man and was hospitalized many times during my early years. Heart and lung disease were taking their toll on him; according to Mum it was a combination of a natural predisposition and the legacy of his service during the Second World War. Taking time off school to go and visit Dad in hospital was becoming a regular event, and I longed for the day when he would be back home again. With the luxury of hindsight and the perspective of being a mother myself I can only imagine how difficult it must have been for Mum to manage on her own at these times. But manage she did.

In the August school holidays, when I was in year three, my beloved father passed way. He went to hospital one night and he never came home. Although he had been unwell, he was not expected to die. My mother was left with a 13-year-old and an eight-year-old to raise single-handedly. I was devastated by this news; how could I be left with *her*? Why couldn't she have died

ONE | In the beginning

instead of Dad? My eight-year-old brain tried to process what I saw as a great injustice and surely some kind of mistake. And so, I received the lesson very early on in life that things don't always go to plan, and that you have to find a way to go on when the worst happens.

My dad's funeral was a curious affair for the eight-year-old me. Mum did a fairly good show of holding it together, but she was understandably distracted. While we waited in the church for the service to begin Mum handed me to Cora, her cousin's wife, and told me to stay with her. Clearly Mum had a few things to attend to before the service began and it would be more manageable without me tagging along. Cora held my hand and smiled at me, she was a lovely warm woman, and I was more than happy to be with her. We sat and waited patiently on a pew with others near the back of the church. Then, without warning the funeral began. I was safe with Cora, but I wanted to be with my Mum and my brother Euan sitting in the front pew. *Why didn't Mum come to get me? Has she forgotten about me? Dad will think that I don't care if I'm not sitting at the front.* I was far too shy to walk up to the front by myself, yet that's what I desperately wanted to do. I was always being told to speak only when spoken to, so I didn't say anything to Cora, lest I get into trouble from Mum for speaking during the service. I remember nothing about the service itself, as I was too confused to take any of it in. I felt trapped but was powerless to do anything about it; so, I did nothing, I made no sound, and did not move a muscle even though my heart was breaking.

The fights between my Mum and my brother escalated after Dad's passing. Now she had to be both father and mother, and the iron fist she ruled with grew even tighter. Staying out of the way became more important than ever now that Dad wasn't there to soften Mum's tempers. By now I had mastered the fine art of being invisible and I was using it to my best ability.

After Dad's passing, surprisingly, most things remained unchanged. To her credit Mum kept our lives as similar to before as possible, so with the exception that Dad was now gone, everything else stayed the same. We remained in our home, we attended the same school, kept the same friends, lived in the same community. Somehow, I *knew* that life would get better, I just knew it would. And so, life went on.

ONE | In the beginning

Learned wisdom

- The police and other authorities and government agencies take domestic violence seriously
- Just because you may not have a black eye or a split lip it does not mean that you are not being abused
- If you can articulate your experiences and be honest about what you have endured, you have more chance of being heard
- Abusers are often selective about how they choose their victims, don't underestimate how your childhood experiences can influence this

TWO | A fine romance

Fast-forward eighteen years and I was a young woman living life to the full. I was no longer the painfully shy child hiding her face in her mother's skirt. Secondary school had knocked most of the bashfulness out of me. Compulsory public speaking and speech and drama lessons meant that I could give the illusion of being confident and engaging on cue.

I left home as soon as I turned eighteen to start my own life free from the constant bickering in the family home. Unlike Euan's preference for it, confrontation had never been my friend. Deep down I was still a 'good girl' who didn't want to get into trouble; it was so much a part of my DNA, and so ingrained in my psyche that it defined me.

By now I was living in a regional city and working in the media as a sales executive, a sometimes-glamorous job that I loved utterly. I took to country life like the proverbial 'duck to water'. It was reminiscent of my childhood living on the outskirts of a capital city. There was room to breathe, wide-open skies and a sense of community that welcomed you even if you were a newcomer.

THE GILDED CAGE

In time I was encouraged by locals-with-influence to represent my adopted city in a quest to raise funds for medical research. When I say quest, I mean Quest with a capital Q, as in a competition where young ladies are judged on merit, personality, confidence and service within their community. I entered because it seemed like a good idea at the time, and I didn't want to 'disappoint the locals'. It was through the heats to the finals and, somehow, I was crowned overall winner. I had the sash, the tiara, and now the title; an overseas trip, clothes, jewellery and other wonderful rewards were part of the prize package. This was the opposite of being invisible (my place of safety as a child) but, as I was all grown up now, I thought I could handle the attention.

My win gave me some minor-celebrity status in a small regional city where celebrities were thin on the ground. It was a natural consequence that I found myself on the judging panel for the next year's quest. The panel consisted of the usual suspects: community leaders, council representatives, and business luminaries. When I was fundraising for the quest I came into contact with a good chunk of the town's population, whether I was asking for donations, selling tickets, or promoting events. Interestingly I had made a conscious decision not to approach

TWO | A fine romance

the biggest and most notorious player in town. Funds had been raised and the profile of the quest had been elevated without his help, thank you very much. It's curious as to why I kept a wide berth, but I think it was a case of me listening to my inner voice for once. ***Stay away, there's danger there.***

But it was harder to dodge the previously avoided business 'luminary' now that we were together on the judging panel. I was aware of his presence, but fortunately I was sitting at the other end of a long table and I was out of his direct gravitational pull. He was an out-of-the-ordinary creature in a whiter-than-white country town. From Eastern Europe he was dark, exotic, sophisticated, self-assured, successful and charismatic. The more his presence filled the room, the smaller I felt. I had recently ended a long-term relationship and I was vulnerable, raw and filled with a deep sense of failure. The contents were not the same as those described on the label. My confident, pulled-together façade was wafer-thin, but I held it together well enough to make a passing impression of someone who was poised and self-confident. I don't remember a great deal about the judging process, but I managed to get through it and made a discreet and early exit from the event.

THE GILDED CAGE

A few days later I was working in my office at the local radio station when the receptionist called out from the front office, "Artur Zaczek is on the phone, can I put him through to you?" It was a busy day and I was distracted; "Yeah, sure," I responded vaguely. I sat up when I heard the voice at the end of the line. It was deep and with an unmistakable European accent: mysterious, and curiously unsettling. Despite my efforts to avoid contact, the business luminary had tracked me down. Artur's commercial empire was vast, and he owned several businesses along the eastern seaboard. It was a multi-million-dollar enterprise and it represented advertising revenue that the radio station had long given up on attracting. It would certainly have been a significant achievement if I could have secured that account.

Artur explained that he was looking at advertising on the radio station I worked for and he would like to meet with me – over lunch. It was the late eighties and in the heady world of advertising much business was done over long lunches, so this was nothing out of the ordinary. We arranged to meet at one of the better restaurants in the area the following day.

TWO | A fine romance

When I arrived at the agreed time there was only one other car in the car park; it was a large Mercedes-Benz sports coupe, and I rightly presumed it was his – well there weren't too many of them in our neck of the woods. He was already at the table, smoking (I did say it was the eighties, didn't I?) and drinking whiskey. This was not the most appealing sight I had ever seen, but as I was only there to sign him up, I could live with it. I was well prepared for the meeting, and while we waited for our meals, I brought out rate cards and general information to help him decide which advertising package would be best for his business. Although I tried to keep the topic of the conversation professional, Artur deftly managed to slip a few personal questions into the dialogue, and I learned that he was sixteen years my senior, divorced, and had teenage sons. It was a pleasant enough lunch, and he was polite, respectful, attentive and engaging. Regrettably, he declined to commit to anything there and then and he told me that he would think about it and get back to me. I was disappointed, but you didn't always get the sale on the day, and at the very least I had laid the groundwork for future sales pitches.

When I arrived back at the office, they asked me how I went; did I get the signature on the dotted line?

THE GILDED CAGE

"No, no success, not this time," I admitted. And immediately there was some good-natured ribbing about being lured to the restaurant under false pretences. I was a bit ruffled by this, as it occurred to me that it might just be the case.

What's that? The imperceptible tinkle of an alarm bell, so faint I can't hear it.

A few days went by and I had given up on securing the Zaczek account as I suspected that he hadn't been genuinely interested in advertising with the radio station. I didn't yet know it, but a man who was accustomed to always getting what he wanted was pursuing me. He was a master tactician and could play the long game with the best of them. I might have thought that I was sophisticated, worldly and experienced, but I was an *ingénue* compared to him. And then Artur made his next move and sent a magnificent bunch of red roses to me at work.

I was more than a little embarrassed by this gesture as our meeting earlier that week had been strictly on a professional basis. Was he feeling guilty for not agreeing to any advertising or was this an indication of something else? He knew that I was courteous and that I would call him to thank him for the flowers. And thus started the manipulation, he was a master

TWO | A fine romance

puppeteer and he was now pulling my strings. Outwardly he was on his best behaviour and continued to behave like a perfect gentleman. There were dinners in lovely restaurants, streams of beautiful flowers sent to the office, and thoughtful gifts, it was all very flattering, and I should have been swept off my feet.

When I was nominated to enter the quest, I was told that I **had** to meet Colleen. She was the person in town who knew everyone, and everything that went on, and she would be invaluable in helping me to fundraise; so, I arranged a meeting with her at the earliest opportunity. She was a tall, attractive woman 'of a certain age' and she had a dynamic energy that you couldn't ignore. She had her finger-on-the-pulse of the town and she did indeed contribute to the success of my fund-raising efforts. Did I mention that she also worked for Artur? Hmm.

Colleen witnessed – no, fostered? – the blossoming romance between Artur and me from the unique perspective of working for one, and befriending the other. One day, some months after Artur and I had started dating, Colleen and I had coffee together. We were now close friends, and I confided to her that I was having second thoughts about Artur and that I was thinking of ending the relationship. It was fun, but I just couldn't see a future in it. The age and cultural differences were not inconsiderable, and I was becoming more and more aware of them as time went on. I was surprised by how earnest her response was.

She urged, "You can never have enough friends, and he can be a good friend to you, so don't cut yourself off from that at the very least."

Tinkle, tinkle, a little louder this time, but I can't hear it over the sound of bad advice.

Years later, I would reflect on this exchange and how different my life might have been if that conversation had ended differently. Or if I had listened to my inner voice and disregarded the 'advice' I was given. If I was cynical, I could say that Colleen might have been acting out of self-interest and that influencing me to stay in a relationship with this man was to her advantage. The truth is I should have acted on my misgivings and made the decision myself, without seeking the counsel of others. But that's what we do, isn't it? We talk important things over with friends to make sure we are considering our decisions

TWO | A fine romance

fully. And so, I didn't end my relationship with Artur, and life would never be the same.

THE GILDED CAGE

Learned Wisdom

- Listen to your inner voice – if something doesn't feel right, it probably isn't
- Be careful of 'advice' from people who may have a hidden agenda

THREE | Into the gilded cage

Life was pretty good. I had work I loved, a wonderful man who was smitten with me, and I was young, with my whole life ahead of me. One evening, Artur and I had plans for dinner at the best restaurant in the area. It faced onto a lovely park in the centre of town, and as we had arrived a little ahead of time, he suggested we take a stroll around the park first. As we walked together, he slowed down and started talking nervously, which was unusual for him. He was always in charge, in total control of himself and his surroundings.

It suddenly dawned on me that he was about to propose to me; I wasn't expecting this, and I was momentarily knocked off balance. As I started to process what he was saying and doing, I saw that he was standing in front of me with a ring box in his hand, not exactly on one knee but the picture was pretty clear. He moved to open the ring box and I stopped him. I presumed that the content of the box was going to be spectacular and I didn't want it to influence my answer. If I was going to say yes, it needed to be without being dazzled by a sparkling diamond. I was only too well aware that he was a very wealthy man and I knew that there would be those who would accuse me of marrying him for his money. And so, I did say yes, and Artur looked relieved and happy. When I opened the box, I found an exquisite ring set with a beautiful 2-carat solitaire diamond. It was a simple and elegant award-winning design made by an eminent local jeweller.

During a surprisingly candid conversation before we were married, Artur told me that his business was under stress and that there was a chance he may lose everything. I was shocked to hear this, but I was grateful for his honesty. He explained that large borrowings to fuel the rapid expansion of the business portfolio, and high interest rates, were making his position vulnerable. I was a young woman in love, and I assured him that I would be marrying him 'for richer or poorer' so it didn't matter what the future held as long as we were together. And I meant every word of it.

Our wedding was to be a simple affair, and at Artur's suggestion we eloped to an island to get married and have a short honeymoon. I was disappointed that both our mothers would not be there, and they were disappointed too. I didn't mind it being a simple wedding, but I would have liked our families there to share the occasion with us. But this was what

THREE | Into the gilded cage

he wanted, and sadly it guaranteed that our wedding anniversaries were never an occasion for our families to celebrate: just a painful reminder that we left them behind.

We flew in Artur's own plane to an island off the coast of Australia to be married at a private resort. His pilot was the best man and the owner of the resort was my attendant. We were so many miles from home and yet we had nobody else we knew or loved with us to share what should have been a joyous occasion. It was a bittersweet moment. With the clarity of 20/20 hindsight, I believe this was the first step in isolating me from my family and friends.

Click, the door on the gilded cage shuts and I am locked inside.

After we were married, we moved to a house on an acreage plot on the edge of town. There were neighbours in the distance, but not so close that you could hear them, nor could they hear you. It was a lovely comfortable country home, spacious but not ostentatious, with a riverfront location and sweeping rural views. It was a little slice of paradise. A few sheep and some horses on agistment kept the paddocks tidy, and fragrant rose bushes surrounded the homestead. I was not involved in the purchase of the property because, as Artur explained, he was 'a businessman' (a phrase he would roll out anytime he would want to inflate his own sense of self-importance) and I was not to worry myself about such matters. Years later I would discover that I was not named on the title deed to the property, something that would both disappoint me and come to protect me.

The first openly ugly episode happened a few months after we had moved into our new home, while my mum and step-dad were visiting. My relationship with my mother had matured as I had matured, and with the independence of adulthood I no longer feared her. I now enjoyed her company and I loved my step-dad, Bob, as I always felt that he was 'in my corner'. Their time with us on this occasion was joyous, as they had come to celebrate that I was expecting a baby, which would be the first grandchild for my mother. My mother-in-law had also joined us for lunch, and we were all sitting outside on the veranda afterwards when the conversation turned to the curtains I was making for our new home. I had purchased a sewing machine and an overlocker, not particularly upscale ones but good enough to make furnishings for the home and the nursery, and clothes for the baby. I was no couturier, but I was a fair home-

THREE | Into the gilded cage

sewer and more than capable of turning my hand to making curtains and baby clothes so we could save a few pennies.

What erupted next was inexplicable. Artur started screaming at me for wasting money on the sewing machine and overlocker. In his vitriolic diatribe he accused me of spending $1000 on a sewing machine. I was bitterly hurt and confused by this attack, and through tears I tried to remind him that the machine and the overlocker together had not cost that much, and that he had approved the purchase. He stormed off and walked through the paddock down towards the river and immediately Bob followed to 'have a quiet word with him'. In shock, my Mum and I sat with gaping mouths, trying to make sense of the outburst. I knew that my mother-in-law was embarrassed by her son's behaviour, and as the afternoon was ruined now, Mum and Bob left as soon as they politely could.

As they drove off, I asked myself, "Who is this man?" I didn't recognise him as the man I married. Unfortunately, Artur's fit of temper that day was just a small taste of his future conduct.

Never again did Artur attack me like that…in front of witnesses. All future tirades, and there would be many more, were strategically carried out in private. I was lucky that day; I had witnesses and a stepfather who wasn't afraid to stand up to a bully. Clearly, I was not yet isolated enough.

Artur and I put the episode behind us, and the months passed by without further incident, primarily because (without realising it) I was doing whatever it took to keep the peace. Keeping busy helped, and one of the benefits of living in the country was a busy social life. Country folk have a way of keeping their calendar full, possibly because they have to make their own fun. One evening, not long before our baby was due, we were at a social gathering with most of our friends, when someone asked me if we had chosen names for the baby yet. We had elected not to know the gender, so we discussed 'if it's a boy the name is...' and 'if it's a girl the name is...' "Wow that's very definite," said my friend. And before I could answer, Artur responded, "Well it has to be as she's only going to have one child." He delivered this bombshell with his most charming smile. You could have cut the air with a knife. No one knew where to look. I felt ashamed to be humiliated so publicly, and the look on my face would have shown it. How brave of him to drop this on his heavily pregnant wife in front of her friends. He knew damn well I would not dispute this or discuss it in public. Another unilateral decision: Artur 1, me 0.

THREE | Into the gilded cage

This new information was an eye-opener; naturally I had presumed that we would have more than one child. It had never been my intention to only have one child, I saw us as a family with children, not a family with a child. Somehow the conversation moved on and I was grateful not to be part of it. It was taking all my energy to keep smiling while my heart was breaking. Another autonomous decision, this was becoming a habit. By now I knew better than to question Artur's decisions unless I wanted to enter into a raging argument with him. The little girl who hated being in trouble, who avoided confrontation at any cost, was still there just below the surface, scratch and you would find her. But now it was becoming clear that avoiding confrontation was coming at a very high price.

THE GILDED CAGE

Learned Wisdom

- Domestic violence often starts once the perpetrator feels secure in the relationship, for instance after the couple are living together, are married, or have children
- The perpetrator believes that the victim is unlikely, or unable, to leave them once they have the responsibility of children or other shared obligations

FOUR | A 'charmed' life

I had resigned from my much-loved position at Artur's suggestion; or was it at his insistence? It's so hard to remember sometimes. He reasoned that there was no need for me to work now with a baby on the way. So, for the next few months after leaving work, I busied myself with preparations for the new arrival and in creating a home out of our new house.

I was blessed with an easy pregnancy and it seemed to pass in a blink of an eye. Our darling baby boy arrived three days early, and with a minimum of fuss, the same way that he would continue on in this world: happy, healthy and easy-going. When the midwife placed the most adorable baby in the world in my arms, it was love at first sight. I was utterly lost in those exquisitely big, beautiful eyes looking up into mine. He would make everything that I was to endure at Artur's hands bearable. We named this wonderful little creature Tim. He was a placid child, and I quickly tired of listening to other babies cry through the night when mine was soundly asleep. I wanted to leave hospital and take my baby home, but in those days, and especially in a country maternity ward, you stayed in for a minimum of five days. I might have had a chance of going home early if this had not been my first baby, but first-time mums stayed the full duration, no matter what. I certainly wasn't going to argue the point with a country hospital matron!

Soon enough I was home and Artur and I settled in to life with our new baby. He was an experienced father and was no stranger to the realities of raising children, yet he made no attempt to help with nappy changing. Despite encouragement from me he declined my offers and made it very clear that he would not be changing any nappies, thank you very much. In fairness to him, Artur did change a nappy once when I was taken suddenly very ill and nearly collapsed in the middle of changing one. I could feel myself falling and called out urgently for him to help me, as I held on to the changing table for dear life. He could tell that it was an emergency from the panic in my voice and he came and took over. He had no trouble changing the nappy, in fact he did a great job, so it wasn't a lack of ability that was stopping him. It was just another strategy to remind me who was the boss.

With the possibility of the business failing at the back of my mind, I was committed to running our home economically and efficiently. There were no extravagances, and I made only sensible and considered purchases. Common sense dictated

FOUR | A 'charmed' life

that I cooked meals from scratch and sewed clothes for the baby and me wherever possible. Bargains were purchased on lay-by, and I bought nothing on credit. Well, I certainly wasn't going to be given access to a credit card! If I didn't have the cash, I couldn't afford it.

A small allowance was paid into my bank account every week. I was expected to make the money stretch, and it was only with judicious budgeting that I could make ends meet. I had watched my mother prudently manage money all through my childhood. Memories of her sitting at the dining table with a little black cash tin, notes and coins, writing figures in neat columns on a piece of paper left a lasting impression on me. With her pen and paper, she would make a dollar go further than anyone else could. If she could do it, so could I.

So, even though we looked like an affluent family, there was no money for *me* to squander. But, of course, there were exceptions. Artur still drove his expensive European sports coupe, and this was 'perfectly acceptable' as he reminded me at every opportunity that he was a businessman and the car was leased through the company. In contrast, I drove a compact Japanese sedan. Now don't get me wrong, it was a perfectly good car and I was grateful to have it. Yet the message here was loud and clear: I would make do with a small car, fine for a baby, pram and shopping, and he would drive around in a large powerful marque for just one person. There was no ambiguity about who was in charge.

I had a small but wonderful circle of friends, and my times with them are among some of my happiest memories from this period. They were other young mums who lived in the same country town. They all had children a little older than my beautiful boy, and provided me with wisdom, love and support in my early days as a new mum. These gorgeous young women were the wives of local business owners, politicians and professionals. The term 'Yummy Mummy' hadn't yet been coined, but you get the picture. Most had put their careers on hold to raise their children and were enjoying being mothers and homemakers for the time being.

It might seem like a contradiction that someone as controlling as Artur encouraged me to maintain these friendships, but there was an ulterior motive behind his generosity. It suited him that his young wife was mixing with the wives of the other

FOUR | A 'charmed' life

important players in town; it enhanced his image and his standing in the community.

The highlight of my week was taking my baby to playgroup; we were just a small crew who met in a community hall. We had assembled a great range of play equipment and the children would play happily together while we watched over them. This circle of beautiful young women was my support group, my base, my girls. We didn't meet in coffee shops for catch-ups, as there wasn't a coffee culture back then. But we did meet up at each other's homes for a cuppa and a chat and so that the kids could play together.

But as much as I enjoyed these outings, I knew better than to stay too long, lest I should arrive home later than expected. It's important to understand that I was always 'allowed' to catch up with my friends, but there would always be a price to pay for it. Thus, Artur could never be accused of actually stopping me from meeting my friends, no – that would be too obvious. It was far better to let me go and *then* make my life hell afterwards if it appeared that I had actually enjoyed myself. This was a shrewd tactic and it was extremely effective in controlling my behaviour. I quickly learnt that if I wanted to avoid his moods or his stony silences, I would need to modify my behaviour accordingly. And modify my behaviour I did. If it meant not having him yell at me and deliver his vitriolic tirades around a small child, so be it.

To the casual observer, it would have appeared that we led a charmed life. We were regulars on the invitation lists to the Mayor's Ball, picnic races, dinner parties, art exhibition openings and all the must-do social events. We lived in a beautiful home and (one of us) drove an expensive car. The reality was nothing like the illusion: I was a scared young woman living in a gilded cage. In truth, I lived a life of apparent luxury, but I had little freedom.

Charmed life or not, it was certainly an unusual one. I had experiences that never touched my friends' lives. About a year after we were married, Artur received notice from the Australian Tax Office (ATO) that he would be required to undergo a tax audit. It was possible that this was no random event, but he explained it away by insisting that the ATO 'had it in' for successful businessmen like him. Well, you had to give him credit, he was nothing if not self-assured. Correspondence received from the ATO indicated that I would be examined as

FOUR | A 'charmed' life

part of the audit, and that I would be required to attend an interview.

At the appointed time I turned up for my interview, in the boardroom of Artur's business headquarters. I had been unable to secure a babysitter, so I had Tim with me. I can assure you that having an energetic toddler with you while a tax auditor is grilling you is less than ideal. But then again, I was becoming accustomed to living a life less ordinary. I found myself being asked a series of questions from a checklist by a tax auditor straight out of central casting. He was conservatively dressed and had a serious demeanour and I could tell that he was not thrilled about the toddler being present, but then again neither was I. To be fair to him he was clearly trying to make this experience less of an ordeal for both of us. I was naively unconcerned, as I had nothing to do with Artur's business enterprises and didn't feel that I had anything to worry about. I was asked if any assets or property had been transferred to my ownership in the previous twelve months. Fat chance! I was also asked, among other things, about overseas holidays, expenditure and income. Income! Well, my little allowance wasn't going to raise any eyebrows was it? In between wrangling a two-year-old who was simultaneously climbing

THE GILDED CAGE

under the table and trying to sit on my lap, I answered the questions put to me and with each answer the auditor ticked a box, and sometimes made additional notes. Eventually the assessor finished ticking all the items on his checklist and thanked me for participating so cooperatively. In some respects, I was really puzzled as to why I had been interviewed, but then again, my life hadn't been normal by other people's standards for a long time. In due course I received a letter from the ATO advising me that they were satisfied with their investigation and that there was no further action required. Phew! Artur was also found to be in the clear, and I could only think that some people were covered in a non-stick coating – nothing stuck.

When our son was two years old, Artur announced that I would be co-managing one of the retail businesses. We'd had previous discussions about me going back to work, but I was told in no uncertain terms that it would be unseemly for me to work for anyone else but him, given his standing in the community. My sister-in-law already ably managed part of the operation and I was being drafted in as partner to help her. Artur had decided that they needed a new strategy to protect a portion of the business from the reach of any potential receivers. The threat of the business being taken was ever-present, and one of the retail

FOUR | A 'charmed' life

arms of the enterprise could be quarantined if my sister-in-law and I formed a legal partnership, leased it, and ran it 'independently'. Nevertheless, we were expected to run the business efficiently and profitably, and we did. I worked part time on the floor and did the bookkeeping at home when I could snatch time while my toddler was napping. It was good to be back at work, but it was also challenging, as I had never before been a bookkeeper.

And while it might seem that my new role would give me some independence, there was no doubt that we were both working for 'the firm'. I received a small income, but naturally my allowance was reduced proportionally.

After work one evening, I had made dinner and I was waiting for Artur to come to the table so I could serve the meal. After a few minutes had gone by, and not wanting the meal to get cold, I decided to go and find him. I looked everywhere in the house first, but he was not there. I checked outside and still could not find him, but then I heard a noise coming from the garage. In the dim light I could see that it was Artur and I called out, "There you are, dinner's ready."

THE GILDED CAGE

As the words left my mouth, I could see that I had caught him off guard. He was drinking heavily from a bottle and choked and spluttered as he turned towards me. He yelled, "What the hell are you doing here, don't sneak up on me like that!"

I replied, "Why are you drinking in the garage? Do you need a drink that much?!"

Well, that wasn't a smart thing to do. The fact that I had caught Artur drinking and then challenged him about it was too much. I had overstepped the mark, and I knew it. A spleen-venting tirade followed about how I should mind my own business and if he wanted to have a drink in the garage, he would do it. Considering how much he drank openly in the home, I wouldn't have thought that he would need to drink anywhere else as well. But how wrong I was.

Many years later, when this particular incident came up in a private conversation between Tim and me, he revealed that he had also walked in on his father having a sly drink in the garage at home. Tim was about ten years old at the time and was a little bewildered by what he witnessed and, given his age, he had no understanding of the implications of it. In hindsight, it was evident that Artur's surreptitious drinking continued as a

FOUR | A 'charmed' life

pattern of self-destructive behaviour throughout our marriage and beyond.

One of the reasons Artur's clandestine drinking had gone unnoticed by me for so long was because I was anosmic – that is, I had no sense of smell. This placed me at a great disadvantage as I could never smell alcohol on his breath and he knew it. How perfectly advantageous it was for him.

It was beginning to dawn on me that Artur might have a drinking problem, and how that might contribute to his erratic temper and belligerent behaviours. So often it was in retrospect that the pieces of the puzzle fell into place, and this now made sense of an incident that had taken place some months beforehand. We had decided to take a trip travelling by car north along the east coast so we could combine business and a brief holiday with a toddler in tow. Calling into his sites on the way, we would take care of business first and then drive on to Queensland for a small vacation. On this particular day we had pulled in to a roadhouse for a short break from driving and to have some lunch. As we reached the restaurant, he remembered he had left something in the car and had to go back for it, and he told me to go ahead and order. We had a pleasant enough lunch and then all got back into the car to continue on our way. No sooner had we merged on to the highway than a police car pulled us over, lights and sirens going. I was really puzzled by this as we had just left the roadhouse and certainly weren't speeding, as there hadn't been time for the car to accelerate to the speed limit. The police officer performed a random breath test on Artur, which he passed, and again we continued on our journey. At the time I thought how curious it was for the police to inexplicably stop the car for a breath test in the middle of the day. Sometimes you just can't see what is in front of you.

Years later I would become painfully aware of just how dependant on alcohol Artur was. By chance one day while looking for one of Tim's toys that I thought must have been dropped in Artur's car, I discovered a bottle of scotch, his drink of choice, under the passenger seat. It was wrapped in a t-shirt, presumably so it would not bump and make noises when the car was travelling. Having the bottle under the passenger seat meant that when Artur was alone he could easily access the bottle for a quick drink while sitting in the driver's seat. Once I discovered his little secret I discreetly checked to see if it was a regular thing, or perhaps it had just been left there by mistake. I soon learned that the bottle was changed every day or so!

FOUR | A 'charmed' life

I now understood why he was always adamant to clean his own car and unpack anything from it himself. I thought he was just being selectively helpful. More fool me!

So now I realised that the police 'randomly' pulling him over for a breath test in the middle of the day was no accident. The police car had been parked at the roadhouse and I can only presume that the officers had observed Artur having a sly drink in the car when he went back to get whatever it was that he had 'forgotten'. This was a dangerous habit that he was concealing for obvious reasons, it would do his image no good to be labelled a drunkard.

It made my blood boil! How many times had Artur driven under the influence of alcohol? What sort of danger did he pose to himself, to me, to Tim and to other road users? From that point on I quietly made sure that I did the bulk of the driving, as I didn't want Tim in the car with a drunk driver. I 'kindly' volunteered to drive each time we went out socially, and Artur was happy with this as it meant that he could drink and not have to worry about keeping under the limit. Looking back, it's amazing that Artur didn't get booked for driving under the influence. Perhaps his habitual drinking protected him from registering high breath-alcohol concentrations. But then again, if he had been caught, he wouldn't have told me about it, and given his now-evident talent for subterfuge he was more than capable of hiding anything from me.

FOUR | A 'charmed' life

Learned Wisdom

- A woman doesn't need to be hurt physically to suffer abuse and domestic violence. While emotional and financial abuse leave no physical scars, they can deeply scar mental health and wellbeing. Anxiety, depression, and even suicide can be the outcome for women experiencing emotional, financial and other abuses
- Be vigilant for the signs of financial control: scrutinising what the victim spends money on; finances entirely controlled by the dominant partner; secrecy regarding income and expenditure; failing to provide adequate living expenses; and preventing a woman from working outside the family business, if at all
- Abusers use non-physical domestic violence to assert control in the relationship by stripping the woman of her freedom, confidence and self-respect
- Non-physical domestic violence is often unseen by others, and can continue for a very long time without detection

FIVE | The winds of change

Four years after we were married, the inevitable happened, and the receivers took control of Artur's business assets. Market conditions had not improved, and the over-extension of his borrowings meant that his financial position did not recover sufficiently to survive the banks calling in their loans. The winds of change were blowing our way, and we could do nothing to stop them. This was a wretched and taxing time: we now faced the very real prospect of losing the businesses and our home. However, in dark moments, it's often the mundane that gets you through.

That evening, with the weight of the receivers' intent on my shoulders, I kept myself occupied with my regular nightly chores. I watched the evening news on television as I made Tim's lunch to take to day-care the next day. I can still see clearly in my mind the images on the screen covering the famine in the Democratic Republic of Congo. The pictures of hungry and malnourished children sitting quietly in the dirt still affect me to this day. Their desperate mother sat hopelessly beside them, with nothing to feed them. And here I was fretting about losing material possessions, but I still had enough food for my child. It was a surreal experience and it made a lasting impression about how much mine was a First World problem, and how other people all around the world were facing issues which made mine pale into insignificance.

By this time, I was an expert at keeping up appearances, so I kept up the pretence of everything being normal. No doubt the rumours would have spread around town about our situation with the receivers, yet people were exceptionally kind and considerate, to me at least. They would have known that we were losing nearly everything, yet they did not make an issue of it. People can be far more generous than we give them credit for. I was only able to talk about the loss with my closest friend, and even then, it was only with the sketchiest of details. The receivers took what they needed to cover the debts, and so the businesses were taken, and our home was taken. We were able to keep our furniture, and I kept my little car. Artur's car had to go, and what did he replace it with? Another Mercedes-Benz sports coupe, naturally. Admittedly this one was a few years older than his original one, but you have to admire some people, they don't give in easily, do they?

FIVE | The winds of change

As a consequence of the bank recalling their loans and appointing receivers, Artur was declared bankrupt and eventually so was his eldest son. It seemed a peculiar and unnecessary action to declare a young man bankrupt, and I didn't understand why it happened. When I questioned both of them about it, Artur reluctantly told me that the family home had been purchased in his eldest son's name as a way of quarantining the asset from any potential creditors. Artur's eldest son was eighteen when the house was purchased and would have had no means with which to purchase the property, so this was a blatant sham. While I had been disappointed and upset at not being named as an owner of the house, Artur's sneaky little subterfuge actually protected *me*, but it would come back to bite *him* in later years. I was exempted from any of the bankruptcy actions, ironically, because Artur deemed that I was unworthy to own any assets.

However, now I was a more useful commodity, because as an undischarged bankrupt he had certain restrictions placed on him. For instance, he had to relinquish his passport and was not permitted to leave the country for the three-year term of the bankruptcy. Additionally, he was unable to obtain finance, and applying for new accounts with utilities providers was virtually impossible as most application forms ask the applicant to declare if they are, or have ever been, bankrupt. This didn't bother him much; he was more than capable of being selective with the truth when it suited him.

So, from this time on any new accounts (that I was aware of) were applied for in my name only. This was proof that I was useful enough when it suited Artur, but I was still unworthy to own, or co-own, any assets or shared wealth. It said everything about how little Artur valued me and showed a pattern of behaviour I would learn to recognise.

For the time being, we continued to manage one of the retail concerns because the receivers were satisfied to keep it operating under their ownership while they found a purchaser. This was the only source of income for us now, and it was a peculiar experience to be working with your husband one day, and then working with receivers the next.

So, what do you do when you lose your business and your home? You move to Queensland, of course. Another unilateral decision made by Artur, as no discussion with me was apparently required. We had holidayed a couple of times on the Gold Coast and he determined that Queensland was where we

FIVE | The winds of change

should be. Moving such a long distance was an enormous wrench for me. At that time my mother lived about an hour and a half away from us by car, and this was manageable for the two of us. I would visit her every fortnight and we would do her shopping together and have some lunch out and she would enjoy some time with Tim. She and I both looked forward to these outings together, but this would no longer be possible if we were so far apart.

I would miss my mother-in-law too. We had formed a genuine and loving bond and I hated the thought of leaving her behind. I am certain she must have had some idea how difficult her son was to live with, yet it remained only an unspoken understanding between us. She looked after Tim sometimes when I worked and often when I picked him up from her she would have a home cooked meal ready for me to take home. I was more than happy to repay the kindness in any way that I could, mostly by accompanying her to her medical appointments or helping her with correspondence, as English was her second language.

So, it was with a heavy heart that I left my beloved country home to move far away. The busyness of packing up and relocating and finding my feet in a new location kept me sane through that dark time. Moving into a rented home, finding a suitable pre-school for Tim, learning where the local shopping centre was, finding a doctor – were all routine tasks that kept me occupied and prevented me from dwelling on any sense of loss. My focus now was on setting up a safe and secure family home and making the transition as smooth as possible for all of us, especially Tim.

Fortunately, Tim was still young enough not to be bothered by the move too much, and he settled in to his changed environment and made new friends with apparent ease. Unfortunately, Artur's drinking showed no signs of diminishing and I was constantly 'walking on eggshells' trying to second-guess his moods. I needed to keep him as happy as possible so that peace could be maintained at home. No doubt the loss of his businesses had weighed heavily on him, but he took it surprisingly well, too well in fact. Did he know something that I didn't?

Jingle, jingle. The warning bells were a little louder now, but I was too busy starting a new life to pay them any heed.

FIVE | The winds of change

The income from the retail business was a godsend, but it wasn't going to be enough to cover living expenses in the long term. Peculiarly, a friend of Artur's lent him money to purchase a modest café in a Brisbane suburb. I was taken aback by the generosity of this friend, but Artur assured me that it was not so unusual and that was what 'successful businessmen' did for one another. Hmm. So, we rolled up our sleeves and got stuck in. The café had been closed for some months and was in need of a deep clean and some tender loving care, but we were up to the challenge. After a brief set-up period, we opened the doors, and it was a moderate success from day one. It meant long hours and hard grind, starting early and being on our feet nearly all day. I spent a good chunk of my day loading and unloading the commercial dishwasher, getting drenched in clouds of steam with each load. It was a long way from my glamorous role in advertising, but I comforted myself with the fact that it was good honest work and it enabled us to earn a living, keep a roof over our head and food on the table. It was amazing how liberating it was to lose 'everything'; it helped me to see the world through a new filter of gratitude.

My stepfather Bob had been unwell for some time with serious health issues, and not unexpectedly I received the heart-breaking news shortly after we opened the café that he had passed away. I was grief stricken, both for my mother and for me, and I flew down to Sydney to be with her at Bob's funeral. During the service it occurred to me that he was the one person who stood up for me when I was being bullied by the very man who was supposed to protect me. My loss was palpable, and I sobbed through the entire service. Maybe I was finally able to express my grief for losing my darling father too. Even though people surrounded me, I felt very alone.

The tyranny of distance separated me literally and figuratively from my family and I had never felt more alone than when I returned home to Artur. His moods and outbursts escalated following Bob's death. Perhaps he felt more secure in mistreating me, as no one was going to hold him to account now. My brother Euan lived interstate and was battling his own demons. I knew he was in no position to face up to Artur on my behalf, so I never shared my woes.

Artur's heavy drinking was affecting his behaviour more than ever, relaxing any little amount of self-control he may still have had. He was drinking heavily every day, yet I remained unaware of how big the problem had become. He hid his bottles

FIVE | The winds of change

and disposed of them quickly when they were finished. With hindsight, I believe that he was a high-functioning alcoholic. Even though he drank excessively, he excelled at work and maintained fairly satisfactory relationships with friends and family. But his successes worked against him too, convincing him he had his drinking under control based upon his achievements. It took many, many years for his drinking to finally catch up with him.

What makes living with a high-functioning alcoholic so challenging is that they are often in deep denial about their problem, and this was certainly the case with Artur. I once foolishly used the term 'alcoholic' during one of our heated exchanges. He exploded and rationalised with me just how wrong I was. "Do my hands shake?" he demanded, "No! Am I falling around unable to stand? No! Am I slurring my words? No! You are so stupid; you don't know what you are talking about!"

There was nothing to be gained by pointing out that he couldn't get through the day without a drink, or two, or three, or four… Nor was there anything to be gained by pointing out that behaviours such as deliberately concealing how much he drank by drinking alone, and then hiding the empty bottles, were indicators of a drinking problem. I wasn't going to challenge him and be browbeaten for it; my survival instinct protected me from that much at least. Yet it was my silence that enabled him to continue his drinking unchallenged for so long without consequences for him, but with dire repercussions for those close to him.

FIVE | The winds of change

Learned Wisdom

- Catastrophic changes in circumstances can destabilise the perpetrator. If they feel insecure, they may attempt to control their victim even more so than before
- Alcohol dependence and substance abuse can weaken self-control and escalate the perpetrators abusive behaviour
- If the perpetrator is in denial about their addiction, they may not see a correlation between their controlling behaviour and their substance or alcohol use

SIX | Moving the goalposts

A few years after we bought the café, we had saved enough money for a deposit to buy a home. Having lived in rental accommodation now for so many years, this was an important step, both financially and psychologically. It was a sign that we were recovering from the devastation of losing the businesses and the family home. Artur vowed that he would never be put in the position of having his home taken from him ever again, and so he devised a plan to purchase the home through a third-party trust. He explained that the property would not be in either of our names and would be held in trust on our behalf. However, we would be responsible for paying the mortgage and all other expenses relating to the property.

Artur had two close friends, business professionals, who would create the trust and act as trustees. He assured me that this was the only way that we could purchase a home since his bankruptcy, and like a sucker I believed him. As the trust was purchasing the property, the sale documents went directly to the trustees, but naturally I presumed that Artur and I would be listed as beneficiaries of the trust. This was a grave mistake, and it would come back to haunt me years later.

We purchased a home on a larger than average block in a leafy outer suburb of Brisbane. A respectable house, in a respectable street, in a respectable suburb. It felt good to be in a home of our own again, and I was happy that there were other children living in the street around Tim's age, so he had some ready-made friends from the day we moved in.

But as nice as the house was, slowly and surely my life became even more miserable. Artur's rages, once infrequent, had become regular events. He was escalating their frequency, intensity and duration, and my hope was fading that one day he would just stop behaving this way. There were now more bad days than good days. I convinced myself that if I could be a better wife, a better cook, a better person, a better anything, then perhaps he would be happier, and my life would be happier too. But here's the thing, and it's something that many abusers do: he kept moving the goal posts. So, what made him happy one week would not make him happy the next. It was a deliberate strategy to keep me on my toes, and it worked.

SIX | Moving the goalposts

Every day I was subjected to his criticism chipping away at my sense of self: "That dress does not suit you." "Why is there nothing better in the fridge?" "This meal is not very tasty." "You are too fat." "You are too thin." "Your hair is too long." "Your hair is too short." and so on. I told myself that I would not be broken and that I was strong enough to withstand all of it; I would hold the family together because I refused to fail. I believed that my son deserved better than to be the child of a broken marriage, so pride got in the way of expecting better for myself. I would do anything to hold this fractured family together, and unfortunately Artur knew it. He knew that no matter how poorly he behaved I just would not leave him; I had married him 'for better, for worse, for richer, for poorer'. Well I guess I had those boxes ticked now.

It was an unfair match: the man who thrived on conflict, who in fact was energised by it, and the woman who was a natural peacemaker and mediator. It was never going to be a level playing field, and to be honest much of the time I was just too exhausted to stand up to him.

Shortly after we bought our home, Artur decided we would also open a sweet shop. A cinemaplex was planned for the shopping centre where the café was located, and this would be a strategic fit. A sweet shop would be relatively inexpensive to set up and would be comparatively straightforward to run. So now, I was turned out of the café to run a sweet shop. I had no experience in confectionery retail, but I learnt quickly, as I had no choice in the matter. Long hours on the floor were just the beginning for me. After finishing my shift at the sweet shop, I would pick Tim up from school and then come home to do the bookkeeping for both businesses. I did it all: rosters, payroll, accounts, banking, data entry, reconciliations, marketing, and correspondence. At the sweet shop I also did the buying, merchandising, stock control, and my fair share of hours on the floor. Because our store was located in the cinema precinct, it was required to be open from 9am to 9pm seven days a week, so it was hard grind right from the beginning.

To be fair to Artur he did work hard, but this was limited to his time on the floor; once he left work for the day that was it for him. Not only did I have the bookkeeping for both businesses to look forward to once I got home, there was also the running of the home and the family to attend to: homework to supervise, school lunches to make, cleaning, cooking, washing and ironing, shopping, paying bills and so on. I was so weary that I

SIX | Moving the goalposts

had no energy left to right the wrongs in our marriage. Ensuring I was overworked was an imperceptible and evidently successful strategy to keep me in my place.

During Artur's increasingly frequent tempers, his favourite taunt had become, "The only way you will leave is in a pine box." He often delivered this with his characteristic charming smile, yet it was said with such menace it made my blood run cold. How strange that he should feel the need to say this, as I **never** once mentioned leaving him. I was far too fearful and far too savvy to ever broach the subject. Suggesting marriage counselling was out of the question too, as he saw no problem with our marriage, and why would he? All his needs were being met. Tim and I would dance around his father in a choreography learned through years of sidestepping his black moods and his tantrums. Dodging and ducking had become second nature to us, and we had been doing it for so long that most of the time we were unaware we were doing it.

Sometimes Artur would carry his rage with him and 'park' it for later. He would get home from the evening shift after 10 o'clock some nights and by then I would be sound asleep, spent from the day's activities. Artur would march into the bedroom

THE GILDED CAGE

flick on the light and start yelling at me all over again, picking up where he had left off before heading into work earlier in the evening. He knew I would be disoriented as I struggled to wake from sleep, and he took full advantage. I came to dread the sound of his car pulling into the driveway and hearing the electric garage door rising made my stomach sick with fear.

While I always hoped that deep down Artur loved Tim, he was a lazy and disinterested father at best, and a neglectful one at worst. I was raising my boy as a single parent within a marriage, and I had been for many years. My requests to Artur to be a more involved parent were met with indignation and contempt. He made it clear that he was far too busy, and as I was his mother, Tim was my responsibility. I was convinced that I had done a solid job shielding Tim from his father's lack of interest; after all, it was not his fault that his father was so self-absorbed. So, one Saturday morning I found myself explaining to Tim yet again, "Dad can't make it to cricket today darling, as he has to work". The truth was that Artur was only working for an hour or so and would have had plenty of time to make the match. But remember this was the man who changed only one nappy, so I could hardly expect him to come to a lengthy cricket match, could I?

SIX | Moving the goalposts

What happened next was a defining moment in my relationship with my husband. "Yeah, right!" said Tim, with all the sarcasm a ten-year-old boy could muster. This broadsided me. I was momentarily speechless, so I couldn't find the words to reassure Tim that his father really did want to come to the game. And then, in that split second, I thought, *enough*, no more hiding Artur's poor behaviour. This boy was only too well aware of the truth, and I was not going to be a party to the pretence any more, even if I had been participating in it with the best of intentions.

Jingle, JINGLE, the alarm bells were ringing again and this time I could hear them, only faintly, but I heard them.

Learned Wisdom

- **Exhaustion** is a very effective tool used to control the victim. An imbalance in the division of labour within the relationship is suggestive of this tactic being used
- **Escalation** of violence is typically used when the perpetrator feels they are losing control of a situation
- **'Moving the goalposts'** ensures that the victim can only please the perpetrator temporarily and that they can never feel secure. It is not rational behaviour and it perpetuates the cycle of abuse

SEVEN | Detachment

So that was it, I would no longer cover up for Artur! I had been able to get away with the charade (or so I thought) for so long because Artur was very careful about when and where he victimised me. Up until then, he had limited his most despicable behaviour to times when Tim was not around. I was most in danger when I was home alone with Artur, when there were no witnesses, and no one to defend me. But as his behaviour deteriorated, he no longer bothered to hide it from Tim, so it became the norm rather than the exception. Now Tim was being exposed to the worst of it, and it distressed me to think that he would grow up to think that this was how a woman should be treated. Something had to give, the cycle needed to be broken.

Artur had always tightly controlled the money, so even though we had two small businesses that were trading well, there was somehow never enough money to go around. I earned very low wages, yet I was expected to pay for the home expenses: groceries, phone, electricity, school uniforms, birthday gifts, medical expenses, and so on. My budgeting skills were well practised, yet even I could only make the money stretch so far.

At the beginning of the next school year I was faced with all the usual back-to-school expenses and I was struggling to afford shoes for Tim, so I asked Artur to help with the cost. I explained to him that I needed to buy a pair of black school shoes and a pair of runners, and as Tim had a very wide foot, they needed to be shoes from a specialist shoe store, not shoes from a discount store. Artur looked at me with his usual contempt. "Why can't you manage this with the money you get?" he sneered. I said nothing and I did not move. I was standing in front of him as he was preparing to leave for work. I knew if I tried to say anything now, I would cry and he would despise my weakness as usual, and I would get nothing out of him. So, I continued to stand there, still saying nothing. Finally, he pulled out his wallet and held out a $20 note. "That won't cover even half of it," I explained.

It came out of my mouth before I could help it; this was risky, but I got away with it that time, because he was running late for work, and he wanted the impasse over and done with. He put the $20 note back in his wallet, tossed a $50 note at me, and then

SEVEN | Detachment

stormed out of the door. I breathed a sigh of relief and picked up the $50 note from the floor; it also wouldn't even cover half of the cost of the two pairs of shoes, but it was better than nothing.

The disrespect on Artur's face during that exchange still haunts me to this day. Why did I have to beg for money for school shoes for our son? Surely he should want him to have them? And where the hell was all his money going, anyway? Well, I could account for where some of it was going: his weekly spend on cigarettes and alcohol alone would have been more than enough to feed the family for a week. He alone had the luxury of discretionary spending, although no doubt he would have seen his cigarettes and alcohol as justifiable essentials.

Any previous attempts by me to try to solve the mystery of where his money disappeared had not ended well. If I mentioned how I was struggling financially it would typically lead to what would be a three-day episode. Firstly, it would start with his ranting, screaming, name-calling and swearing. No logical discussion or exchange of perspectives would do for us. The louder he shouted, the more he knew that I would cry and be unable to counter his arguments. The more I cried, the more he despised me. I may have been 'all grown up' now, but I was still that same little girl who hated getting into trouble, who was terrified of conflict. Doors would be slammed, hands would be raised, and he would follow me from room to room yelling at me just to make sure that I got the message. Turn up the volume for maximum impact! Apparently, I was getting what I deserved. The next two days would be a stony silence, a black, bottomless, all-consuming nothingness. The tension would be unbearable, and trying to carry on as if nothing was amiss in front of Tim was draining the life out of me.

I think that the reason I did not identify this sequence of behaviours as domestic violence earlier is because it didn't fit the typical cycle of abuse. There was no actual physical violence in terms of him hitting me, as that would have left evidence of his aggression, and for someone so concerned with his public image that would just not do. I think of it now, rightly or wrongly, as 'white collar' domestic abuse, where the perpetrator exercises control using intimidation, exhaustion and artificial poverty, rather than any physical violence.

Internationally renowned psychologist, Dr Lenore E. Walker developed the social cycle theory known as the Cycle of Abuse

SEVEN | Detachment

in 1979 to explain patterns of behaviour in an abusive relationship. The typical domestic violence cycle is commonly considered to have three phases: the first is often referred to as Tension-building; the second as Incident or Acute Explosion; and the third as Reconciliation or Honeymoon. During the Tension-building phase conflict starts to increase and abuse, be it financial, emotional or verbal, occurs. It may even take the form of spiritual or social abuse. The violence is at its height during the Incident or Acute Explosion phase during which the abuser undergoes a release of tension. This feeling can become addictive and the perpetrator may become unable to deal with anger in any other way. The final phase is the Reconciliation or Honeymoon, which in turn has three separate stages: Stage One is Remorse, where the abuser feels guilty for their actions and may express remorse, and may also try to justify their behaviour by shifting the blame to the victim. Stage Two is Pursuit, where the abuser promises never again to behave violently and may even act kindly towards their victim. Stage Three is Denial, where both the abuser and the victim are in denial about the gravity of the violence and abuse, and continue to ignore the likelihood that the violence could (will) happen again.

THE GILDED CAGE

With Artur, there was no Honeymoon phase. He never once expressed remorse or showed any shame for his actions, nor did he try to pursue me to make things good again. Our denial phase consisted of me being relieved that the worst of a particular episode was over…until the next one, and there would always be another one. After a few days, things would go back to 'normal' and the cycle would begin again. I would be walking on eggshells once more.

Carefully now, step one, step two, step three, and jump.

I did everything that I could possibly do to appease Artur. I worked hard, I kept the house clean and tidy, the washing and ironing up-to-date. I made sure that my hair was styled, that I had makeup on, and my clothes were clean and pressed. It was no small feat on my limited budget; I coloured my hair myself, as I wouldn't dare think of squandering money on a professional colour. Yet no matter what I did it was never enough.

Standards were not allowed to drop, not even for Artur, it seemed. For his part, he kept a neat and tidy garden and lawn, but it was not so that we could actually play on it. It was to be kept perfectly manicured at all times 'for show' and he would

SEVEN | Detachment

not tolerate Tim using it for anything fun like cricket practice. Even though we had plenty of room for it, Tim was not allowed to use the lawn for bowling or batting practice as it churned up the carpet-like turf. I thought that the purpose of a lawn was precisely so that it could be used for backyard games. Some days my anger was so raw that Tim and I would take to the backyard after his father left for work and throw the ball to one another. It saddens me now to think that something as innocent as playing ball in the backyard should be an act of defiance.

Communication between Artur and I became increasingly strained and I was deeply frustrated by my inability to articulate my need for things to improve. And I was exasperated by his inability or unwillingness to listen to me or allow me to have a voice. I considered myself an effective communicator, in fact I took professional pride in my communication skills, so why was I unable to connect with the most important person in my life? Every time we would have a discussion he would shut me down, it wasn't difficult, all he had to do was raise his voice and talk over me. And then talk over me some more, talk a little louder until he was shouting, his face centimetres from mine, walking me backwards until I hit a wall, literally and figuratively. Gulping tears down it was impossible for me to get the words out and I would just give up. Job done. It finally dawned on me that I would never be able to talk meaningfully to Artur this way, and that I would need to find a better way to get a dialogue going without giving him an opportunity to shut me down.

So, I resorted to the one thing I felt most comfortable doing, and that was writing. Writing had been a big part of my day when I worked in marketing. Whether it was writing pitches for sales or copy for commercials, it was all a joy for me, so I decided to write letters to him. They weren't harsh or accusatory, far from it; they were a genuine attempt for me to articulate the things that I believed we needed to improve on. Written in a spirit of love and conciliation, I hoped that he might finally understand how deeply sad I was and what might help to make us both happier.

When Artur asked to speak with me after reading one of my letters, I was hopeful that we might make some progress. I couldn't have been more mistaken! What happened next was reminiscent of being summoned into the headmaster's office for a 'talking to'. He was clearly in no mood to consider the content of my note and gave me a ticking off. The years of heavy

SEVEN | Detachment

drinking and smoking had taken their toll and for the first time I noticed how they had etched his face. As he sat there remonstrating me, he looked like an aged school principal, and I presume his intent was to make me feel like a naughty child. I was in no mood to let him make me feel that way, and as I sat there listening to his diatribe, I accepted that writing letters wasn't going to make him sit up and pay attention, but it did satisfy my need to articulate my needs. Chalk this one up to experience.

Not every attack on my spirit involved shouting and the waving of hands. There were also subtle, subliminal and more finessed tactics deployed as an underlying constant, which were equally effective. Rarely, if ever, was I acknowledged for having a good idea. Quite frankly if I suggested something it was rejected by Artur asserting convincingly, "that is a very bad idea." It didn't matter what the suggestion or notion was, he summarily dismissed it without a moment's consideration. Eventually I came to the realisation that if I proposed something, it was the kiss of death for that objective. If I really felt strongly about something that I wanted to see come to fruition, I had to do one of two things. I could try reverse psychology, whereby I would state the opposite of what I truly sought, with the reasonable expectation that Artur would do anything and everything to thwart what he perceived I wanted. Or, I could plant the seed of an idea knowing that he would refute it immediately, and then (lo and behold!) six months later he would come up with exactly the same idea as his own 'very good idea'.

It was a silly dance of pretence and toxic behaviour, and it was time consuming and energy sapping. Its only purpose was so I would understand that my ideas, goals and intentions were unworthy of consideration, and therefore so was I. It worked to begin with, and it was very effective in eroding my self-confidence, but once I wised up to what was going on, I worked around it as best I could.

For instance, during the Millennium Drought I suggested that a water tank might help us keep the garden watered. During the drought severe restrictions applied to watering gardens, and consequently many beloved gardens failed. In response to this, many homeowners were reinstating water tanks, which had long been out of favour, so that they could use rainwater rather than town water for their gardens. Naturally Artur dismissed this as a 'very bad idea' and nothing more was said. Miraculously, six months later, he came up with the ground-

SEVEN | Detachment

breaking idea that we should consider installing a water tank in our garden. I had a silent chuckle. Well, it was either that or cry.

A few months after Artur's water-tank epiphany, he decided that the time had come to sell the café, as the sweet shop was doing well enough on its own to support the family. The demands of running two labour-intensive businesses had been taking its toll on both of us. Following the sale of the cafe, Artur was now working exclusively in the sweet shop, although never on the same shift as me. Unlike the café, one person could staff the sweet shop most of the time; only during peak times were two staff members required.

Within weeks of Artur commencing work at the sweet shop, I became concerned by the trading figures. Considering the amount of stock I was purchasing, and the mark-up on the products, I figured that our takings should be greater than they were. I had followed the trend for a while just to be sure that it wasn't a short-term anomaly, but the figures weren't improving. I was troubled that the only explanation for it could be staff theft, and this sickened me. We had a few staff members who worked part-time, to give Artur and I some precious time away from the 9am to 9pm seven-day-a-week demands of the business. I placed great trust in them and really couldn't imagine them stealing from us. I discussed my concerns with Artur as I thought this might need to be referred to the police. I was surprised by how dismissive he was of my suspicions.

"You are imagining this, I can't see the staff taking money from us," he declared. I was pleased that he placed so much trust in our staff, but it still didn't explain why the business should not be doing better. He discouraged me from investigating further saying that the business was doing fine, and that my expectations were unrealistic. The busy-ness of running the shop helped to put my disquiet about this to the back of my mind, a place that was becoming a little crowded to say the least.

Clang, clang, clang.

As had become my usual practice I ignored my inner voice, so things went on as usual until an unexpected turn of events. One evening while I was preparing dinner, a quarrel erupted between Artur and me. It was a steamy summer evening and the temperature in the kitchen was about to reach boiling point. I can't even recall what the spat was about, but I certainly remember the incident. It was unusual for me to answer back,

SEVEN | Detachment

because I would end up crying and upset and nothing would ever be resolved during our arguments, but something must have really put a bee in my bonnet that night. I can remember Artur standing behind me and shouting at me as I was chopping vegetables. I couldn't reason with him, but he continued to employ his usual tactic of shouting longer and shouting louder to keep the pressure on me.

Suddenly I spun around to face him, and as I had an extremely sharp 20cm cook's knife in my hand it was now pointing right at his chest. My heart was thumping and all I could hear in that instant was the pounding in my ears. Then I heard someone shouting, "Calm down!" and everything went quiet. I realised that the voice I heard was my own, perhaps a subconscious plea to de-escalate the situation? I had been seconds away from plunging the knife into him, and from looking at Artur's ashen face he knew it too. This episode really rattled me; I now understood how people killed loved ones in the heat of the moment. I was not a violent or aggressive person, and yet I had been all too close to committing a murderous act.

Back to the chopping, focus on the chopping, calm down.

THE GILDED CAGE

I made a decision that night that I would not allow him to drive me to behave that way ever again. And so, my detachment began in that moment. I realised that the opposite of love is not hate. The opposite of love is indifference. Slowly and surely all my love for him had been drained from me, and no matter how much I wanted things to improve, I now knew that they would not. When I cared, he had the ability to hurt me and to control me. But if I didn't love, didn't care, at least he couldn't hurt me emotionally. No more would I cry, because I no longer cared. All the hurtful things he used to say to control me, to belittle me, and to make me feel worthless, would no longer affect me.

SEVEN | Detachment

Learned Wisdom

- The classic Domestic Violence cycle consists of three phases, often referred to as: Tension building; Incident or Acute Explosion; and Reconciliation or Honeymoon
- Understanding it helps to identify patterns of abusive behaviour; this cycle has no place in a healthy relationship
- Be aware that not all abuse follows the classic Domestic Violence Cycle and that there may be variations

EIGHT | Serendipity

It's enlightening to get an outside perspective on your situation and the consequences of your behaviours. My friend Tina pointed out one day that I only ever phoned her when Artur was out of the house and that I used to abruptly end our phone conversations if he came home in the middle of one. This revelation came as quite a shock, and yet Tina was right, that's exactly what I did. She said, "I can tell from the tone of your voice when you pick up the phone if he is home. You are an entirely different person when he is around." Certainly, Artur would be irritated if I was talking on the phone, and not giving him my undivided attention. I guess I thought there was no point poking the bear if I didn't have to! And so, I had unconsciously been phoning my friends when he was not home. I was grateful to Tina for her honesty, but still the truth hurt. How had I not noticed this before? Perhaps it's true; maybe denial is an underrated coping strategy.

In my new disconnected state, I was beyond caring, and because I no longer loved Artur, I was in a much safer place emotionally.

THE GILDED CAGE

And then it took a seemingly insignificant incident to turn my world on its axis, to lift the fog to reveal all.

A week after my conversation with Tina, Artur was taken suddenly ill with a hernia. He was in real and intense pain and it was not possible for him to work. He had emergency surgery to treat the hernia, but it would still be some time before he would be fit enough to return to work. So, we shuffled shifts around at very short notice and everyone worked an extra one or two to cover his absence. I worked on Saturday evening, which was traditionally the biggest night of the week and responsible for a decent chunk of our weekly income. A good Saturday night could make the difference between being able to pay most of the bills or just some of the bills for that week.

Nevertheless, it was an unremarkable night, good solid trading but certainly nothing record-breaking. There were no blockbuster movies showing which would have significantly increased the takings. Yet, at the end of the day's trading when I was cashing up, there was an extraordinary amount of cash in the drawer. Almost double what I would expect for that shift. How could this be? I wracked my brain for an explanation and then, sickeningly, it hit me.

EIGHT | Serendipity

CLANG, CLANG, CLANG the warning bells are deafening and I am made dizzy and unsteady by their din.

The moment had come, I now understood that the income for this evening was nothing out of the ordinary at all, it was perfectly normal. Artur had been skimming the takings, syphoning off money and artificially lowering the turnover. Suddenly, the nagging doubts that I had about the business not being profitable all made sense. So, too, did his insistence that it was nothing to be concerned about or to investigate further. If I had investigated, I might have stumbled on his grubby little secret. I was white with rage! How many times had I cried because there was no money in the business account to pay the invoices, and nothing in the personal account for school expenses? Had the financial hardship of the past many years been manufactured by him? I could never understand how relaxed he was about our lack of funds, but evidently there was no lack for him so why would he be concerned? Where was all this money going? He certainly wasn't spending it on his family! It might not have felt like it at the time, but this awakening was pure serendipity: good fortune in unintentionally finding something valuable.

THE GILDED CAGE

After closing the shop for the night, I sat in my car trying to gather my thoughts and collect my wits. I felt physically ill and I was trying to process how this revelation would influence my future. What should I do about this? Would I confront him and demand an explanation? Or would he just shrug it off in his usual non-stick way? More likely he would be indignant that I could accuse him of such a thing, he would shout loud and long, and our argument would go around in circles until I caved in from exhaustion. And so, I decided I would do nothing, for the moment. I drove home in a fog, stomach churning; I certainly don't remember the trip home. When he asked how the night had been, I said that it had been "Fine, all good". There was nothing more to be said. For now, anyway.

Just to be sure that I wasn't jumping to conclusions I later checked the figures for all shifts that Artur normally worked solo, and compared them to the corresponding figures for the period when he was convalescing. The takings during his absence were well above the figures when he worked. I wracked my brain for anything else that would explain this anomaly, but the only valid explanation was that he was stealing from the cash drawer. Most transactions then were by cash (Eftpos transactions constituted only a small portion of

EIGHT | Serendipity

sales), and cash was easy to skim if you knew how. All he had to do was leave the cash drawer slightly ajar after the previous sale, and then fail to enter the next sale on the cash register but put the cash in the drawer. This would reduce the amount of 'No Sales' (instances of the drawer being opened without a sale recorded) reported on the reconciliation receipt. If this was done often enough, a surprising amount of money could be taken but not recorded, so at the end of the evening when cashing up all he had to do was take out the amount surplus to the total figure and everything would balance.

Artur was sufficiently cunning to record enough sales so as not to arouse suspicion, goodness knows he had been expertly working the system right under my nose for years! So, again I wondered, where was all this money going? Well, that was a question that would have to be answered another day, if ever. Right now, I had other fish to fry.

The first job on my new to-do list was to keep a stiff upper lip. Confronting Artur with my discovery would have been futile, and I had no intention of wasting any time or energy on actions that were pointless. I needed time to think and to consider what was the best way forward from here. Sometimes life makes the decision for you. I can clearly recall the moment when I decided enough was enough and that things would have to change. By that, I mean that *I* would have to change because I knew my husband would not. A life altering decision was made in the most mundane of moments. I had just banked the tell-tale deposit and was sitting on a bench in the shopping centre 'taking a moment' when my mobile phone rang. It was Tina, phoning to say hi and to chat about nothing in particular.

Hearing a friendly voice in that moment made all my resolve crumble and I dissolved into tears. Tina patiently listened as I explained the sequence of events that had led to me sitting in a daze on a bench in a public place. She was a smart cookie, highly educated, and with razor-sharp perception. Apparently, she had Artur figured out from the beginning and could see what I could not. Sadly, she had been watching me for years, waiting for this day to come. She could always be relied upon to look at any situation calmly and analytically and finally she said, "This is abuse, and it has to stop." And there it was, the first time I had heard that word used to describe my husband's appalling treatment of our son and me.

EIGHT | Serendipity

The 'A' word hit me like the proverbial tonne of bricks, and yet it succinctly described all that Tim and I had endured for so many years. The realisation that Artur's treatment of us was cruel, unjustifiable and far from healthy or respectful was a defining moment, and one that would mark the beginning of the next chapter in my life.

Learned Wisdom

- Hiding money or assets from the other partner is unacceptable, and apart from constituting financial abuse, is nothing less than stealing
- Changing behaviours to appease the controlling partner is a typical victim response and the 'thin end of the wedge'.
- Victims will often be unaware that they are modifying their behaviour until it is brought to their attention

PART TWO

NINE | ...and your enemies closer

As I sat there with hot tears falling silently down my face in the middle of the shopping centre, I wasn't feeling self-pity, I was feeling white-hot, seething rage. It was apparent now that Artur had been stealing from the business since its inception and that his insistence on a "simple little cash business" had been with sinister intent. How could this man lie and steal and see the anguish that it caused me, and yet have no remorse? It was over. I would not tolerate being treated this way anymore. I would leave him. In truth, our marriage had been over for a long time and had only survived because I had been artificially keeping it going on life support. It certainly suited Artur to keep the *status quo* as all his needs were being met, but it no longer suited me.

Seeing clearly for the first time in 14 years, it dawned on me that my capacity for self-deception must have been vast. For years I had reassured myself that although Artur was a difficult man to live with, and impossible to keep happy, staying married had been the right thing to do. Over many years, and to no-one but myself, I had trotted out every reason imaginable for remaining in the marriage. It would break his mother's heart; it would

THE GILDED CAGE

break my mother's heart. How could I deprive my wonderful, beautiful son of his father? Who wanted to be a statistic, yet another failed marriage? And yet there were far too many times when I felt truly afraid that I could have been another kind of statistic altogether. So that was it, no more excuses, and no more illogical reasoning. Things were going to change!

Looking back on it all now, it's curious how one person can exercise such control over another human being without ever raising a hand to them. How the threat of harm can be so real, so palpable and so effective that it's enough to put the fear of God into you. It happens in small but increasing increments, so it creeps up on you before you know what has happened. It reminds me of the analogy of placing a frog in a pot of cold water on the stove and gradually turning up the heat until the frog dies. At first the cool water is refreshing and an ideal environment, then as the temperature raises the frog hardly notices the change because the water is still so lovely. By the time the frog is aware that the heat has become unbearable it is too late, the frog is now too weak to jump out of the pot.

When I looked back over the years, I realised how often Artur would make menacing statements just to keep me in line. I recall

NINE | ...and your enemies closer

an occasion when we were watching a documentary on television about the disappearance of anti-drugs campaigner Donald McKay, who was allegedly murdered at the behest of organised crime figure Robert Trimbole. Artur mentioned casually, "There are some Europeans I know who will do whatever you need for a price." And he went on to quote a figure for kneecapping, another figure for a bashing and another figure for murder. When I asked him why he would know this he replied, "I know lots of things, I know lots of people." A seemingly innocent enough statement, but the inference was there. Enough said. By drip-feeding comments like this often enough he made sure that I would think twice before doing anything as foolish as trying to leave him.

Now that I had made the long overdue and life-altering decision to leave, I had to put all this behind me and work out how to get out in one piece. And it wasn't going to be in a pine box! Artur wasn't a man with whom you could have a reasonable and mature discussion about the logistics of exiting a marriage. And I certainly wasn't in a position to ask *him* to leave. As far as he was concerned, it was his house, and no one could make him do anything he didn't want to. I believed that if he suspected that I was intending to leave him, I would end up having an unexplained 'accident'. This was a man who needed to control every aspect of my life in order for him to feel secure. Sometimes it seemed that he even owned the air that I breathed.

No, Tim and I had to leave his father to have any chance of living a fair, healthy and safe life. But first things first, I needed to speak to my Mum about it, so I took a detour on the way home from work that day and called in to see her. By this time, both she and my mother-in-law had moved to Brisbane, and as Mum lived ten minutes away from the family home, I could afford to spend a little bit of time with her without having to explain why I was home later than anticipated. So, I took a deep breath and explained to her the whole sorry mess through sobs and tears. She was shocked to hear how desperately unhappy I had been and how intolerable Artur's controlling behaviours had become. She held my hand and said, "I always knew he was hard on you darling, but I never realised how cruel he had become." I felt wretched for causing my Mum worry, but she was made of stern stuff, and when push came to shove, she was a wonderful ally. She agreed that there was nothing else for it but for me and Tim to find a safer home, and we agreed to talk more about it when we could get more time together. I couldn't

NINE | ...and your enemies closer

stay long, so I cleaned up my face and headed home to prepare the evening meal.

Dinnertime was rarely pleasant, as the slightest thing would irritate Artur and the tension at the table was often excruciating. In later years, Tim confided that his memory of family dinners consisted mainly of his father's argumentative mood, unless we had guests. If we had dinner guests, Artur would be a genial host and behave like a loving father and husband. Maybe I should have invited guests to dine more often.

That night we had an early dinner, as usual, so that Artur could commence the 5pm to 9pm night shift at the store. Naturally I didn't feel like eating, but nor did I wish to arouse suspicion by behaving any differently now. So, with all the will in the world, I mustered up the resolve to eat my meal and join in the talk around the dinner table, no matter how uncomfortable and unnatural the conversation may have been.

Keeping my friends close... and my enemies closer.

Later that night I had a heart-to-heart conversation with Tim, telling him of my intentions to leave his father and giving him the choice to stay if he wished to. The truth is, that if Tim had not wanted to leave, I would not have left without him. He was thirteen years old now, broad-shouldered and tall for his age, with wisdom and maturity that belied his tender years. He assured me that he would be coming with me and agreed to keep quiet about our decision in the meantime. Tim was relieved that we would be starting a new life where we could live under our own terms and not have every aspect of our lives dictated to, and micro-managed, by his father.

Now that the decision had been made, the 'exodus' took on a momentum of its own. Tina had consulted with Paul, a lawyer-friend of hers, about my situation. He was a kind man and, although not a family law specialist, he knew enough to give me some very powerful guidance: "the more you talk about this and let people know what has been happening, the less power he has over you." It proved to be the most important piece of advice I was ever given. Make no mistake, it is the silence that feeds and enables controlling behaviour. Tacit approval is a consequence of not openly naming and shaming. I was raised not to air my dirty laundry in public and unwittingly I had been part of the problem, so now I had to be part of the solution. And so, I did start speaking out. Quietly, one by one, confidential conversations with my friends, during stolen moments over

NINE | ...and your enemies closer

play dates with the kids or strategically timed phone calls. And this is how my 'Ocean's 8' was created, but I'll get to that later.

Tina suggested I get some legal advice pronto from a family law specialist to ensure that I was within my legal rights to leave the family home with Tim. On her advice, I made an appointment to see the foremost lawyer in Brisbane, a named partner in a large firm. In her opinion, I had to have the best advice to take on a wily adversary like Artur. As I had never been allowed to accumulate any money of my own, Mum kindly offered to help to pay the initial legal costs.

So, we concocted a story about Mum having an appointment with a medical specialist in town, and I would take her and accompany her during the 'appointment'. Now I was the one lying about my movements and hiding the truth from my partner. This weighed heavily on me and I shared this with Mum as we travelled into the city together. I confided that behaving in this underhanded way was very uncomfortable for me. I couldn't abide deceit and yet I was now behaving in exactly the way my husband had for years. It was wrong and it was making me physically ill. My Mum was an extremely upright woman with an extraordinary moral compass, and I expected her to agree. She surprised me; she said, "Darling, to catch a fox, you need to think like a fox!" I smiled for the first time in days, and I was grateful for her perspective.

The notion of Mum's specialist appointment was entirely plausible, as I often took my Mum, and my Mother-in-Law, to their respective medical appointments. Both women were well into their senior years and had given up driving, I was often chauffeur and attendant, and happily so. Mum and I met with the lawyer, a man in his middle years who at times seemed distracted, but who nonetheless was knowledgeable. He confirmed that Tim and I were legally free to leave the family home. He also advised that staying in the family home and asking Artur to leave would be preferable, but when he saw the look on my face and my Mum's face at this suggestion he quickly moved on to the issue of when and how we would leave. He understood my concerns regarding safety and agreed that it would be preferable to delay leaving until arrangements could be made for Tim and me to have a safe and secure home to go to. The three of us pored over a calendar, it was now late March, one week to the Easter School holidays; would that be enough time to get organised?

NINE | ...and your enemies closer

I said that leaving during the Easter holidays would be too soon. If I was going to leave on my terms, I would need more time to make arrangements. There was no way I was going to make an eleventh-hour exit taking only what I could grab in haste. I had endured a cruel and dominating marriage, so I was damned well going to control how and when I left. We decided that the June school holidays would be the time to leave. I figured that I could hold on until then, but no longer than that. It was exhausting keeping up the pretence of business as usual and I didn't think that I could last more than a few months. I was being mindful to keep the peace at home and not do anything that would antagonise Artur in the meantime, but it was taking every ounce of resolve I had to do it. If I could just hold on for another thirteen weeks, we would be free.

So now that *when* to go had been sorted, I needed work out *how*. And this is where it got very interesting. I had been encouraged by the support Tina and Mum had shown me, but I was still reticent about sharing my failure with others, partly because I wondered if they would believe me. I had expertly put on a brave face, an Academy Award-winning performance no less, that had hidden the ugly truth for too long. It was time to come clean, and when I did none of my close friends questioned what I shared with them, they accepted the truth for what it was, and they understood the need to keep it in confidence.

It weighed on my mind that when I left Artur I would have no home, no job and no money. ***This wasn't going to be hard at all, then!*** It was evident that Tim and I would need somewhere safe to live and that I would need a new job, as continuing to work in the family business was not an option. It was time to get busy!

NINE | ...and your enemies closer

Learned Wisdom

- The realisation that a relationship is abusive can be devastating. It can take time for the victim to process the implications for themselves, their children and extended family members
- Identifying the abuse and speaking openly about it takes the power away from the perpetrator. Domestic violence flourishes where silence hides the ugly truth
- There are many specific domestic violence support services available these days. They provide discreet, professional and practical support to people suffering domestic violence
- Contact Domestic Violence services for advice and assistance at the first opportunity. If you don't feel safe doing this, ask a trusted friend or family member to do this on your behalf

TEN | The battle plan

Now that I was able to think more clearly and calmly, I formulated a battle plan to exit the marriage in one piece. I'm naturally a fairly organised person and writing to-do lists and executing them was second nature to me. If I could keep the emotion out of the way and plan the exodus like it was any other event, I would be fine. I knew that I would need help, and as my girlfriends had all offered to help me in any way they could, I factored that in to my plans. With only thirteen weeks to D-Day this was no time to let pride get in the way of the objective.

The first thing I did was open a post office box a few suburbs away. I knew I wanted to stay in the area to be close to Mum, but not so close to Artur. Then I organised for all mail addressed to me to be redirected to my new post office box. Artur and I had a post office box ostensibly for the business, but he would always clear it before I could get to it; yet another way he could control my access to information. Now I would get my mail and he couldn't do a damned thing about it! Besides, a secure postal address was vital if I was going to keep my new location confidential. I hid the key for the post office box between the car seat and the car seat cover on the driver's seat in my car. I didn't want to have questions asked about a new key on my key ring!

Then I had to address the issue of how to secure precious memories and the day-to-day things that we would need in our new life. I couldn't bear the thought of leaving behind Tim's baby things or his artworks or even old correspondence. A unit in a storage facility would solve this problem. Tim and I could safely stow treasured belongings until the day came to move out. I didn't want the storage unit to be in my name just in case they ever tried to contact me and blew my cover, so my darling friend Eileen stepped in.

One day, under the ruse of going for a coffee, we instead went to a storage facility that was located conveniently on the way to work for me. Eileen posed as someone looking to rent a small storage unit, and I went as her friend to 'help' her with the decision-making process. We were shown a few sizes, and she would check with me, "What do you think?" I would nod or shake my head, 'advising' my friend of what I thought would suit her best. 'We' decided on a small unit, the size of roughly two toilet cubicles. One day, this would hold the sum total of

TEN | The battle plan

my life. Eileen signed up on the spot and on our way home she handed me the key and the security access code to the facility. Another item to slip under the car seat cover.

Bit by bit I gathered items with which to start our new life. Under the guise of a top-to-toe spring clean, I systematically sorted through all the cupboards at home. After 14 years of marriage, it was amazing how much 'stuff' had accumulated. Of course, there were the precious items: my baby clothes that Mum had lovingly cared for and passed on to me, my son's baby clothes, and a few treasured items belonging to my beloved father. And then there were the practical items: excess Tupperware – who doesn't have that? Crockery, pots and pans, linen, even spare small appliances. The duplicates were astounding, and I felt no guilt packing up items that we had multiples of that I knew Artur would never use. Valuable documents were a priority too: birth certificates, passports, school reports, bank statements, business reports and so on, they all had to be safeguarded.

I had been slowly accumulating some cardboard boxes that the sweet shop stock would arrive in. Instead of throwing them all out, I would keep one or two aside from each delivery, flatten them and hide them in the spare wheel space under the liner in the boot of my car. I didn't want to arouse suspicion by having spare cardboard boxes piling up at home. Each morning after Artur left for work, I would take the flattened boxes out of my car, reconstruct them and pack them carefully with our precious belongings. Then on my way to work I would make a quick stop into the storage facility, stow the boxes, and carry on to work. It was a quick five-minute job each time, but it allowed me to gather a surprising amount of effects that Tim and I would need to start our new life.

The next thing I needed to focus on was the thorny issue of money. So far, the cost of the post office box and the storage rental had been fairly modest and I had been able to manage them with some 'robbing Peter to pay Paul' budgeting. It was clear I was going to need much more to pay for renting new accommodation, some furniture and legal fees – but how was I going to get it? One day, as I was pondering this very question I was looking down at my hands while I was wringing them. And then another bombshell moment happened. I realised that my sparkly, award-winning, two-carat diamond engagement ring no longer sparkled for *me*. Sadly, it no longer represented a lifetime commitment either. I had not asked for this ring, and

TEN | The battle plan

I had always wondered if Artur had purchased it as a status symbol to bolster his image, as much as for any other reason. It had been a beautiful and decorative shackle, but it was now time for it to earn its keep.

My friend Maria owned her own jewellery business and knew several diamond merchants who might buy the stone from my ring. The plan was to sell the diamond and replace it immediately with a cubic zirconia. Maria arranged a meeting, and again under the pretext of a catch up with a girlfriend, I met with her and a diamond merchant. It was a degrading experience, a real low point in my journey to freedom. The merchant examined the ring and made disparaging remarks about the quality of the stone, valuing it for far less than it's insured worth. I knew the provenance of the stone and that it wasn't a piece of junk. But beggars can't be choosers, I was desperate, and this would fund our new start. It was time to let go, so fighting back tears I accepted the amount offered. A replacement stone would need to be sourced, it had to be the right shape, colour and size so that the ring would look the same. In an act of great generosity, for which I will be forever grateful, Maria arranged and paid for the new 'diamond' and booked an appointment for me to see a craftsman jeweller who removed the real stone and set a cubic zirconia in its place. It was a remarkable substitute, all I had to do was keep it clean and it looked just like the real thing. Artur's insistence on keeping separate bank accounts now worked in my favour, as the funds from the sale of the diamond were deposited directly into my personal account.

With some decent money in the bank for the first time, it was now time to organise somewhere to live. While Mum would have sheltered Tim and me, it would have compromised her safety and would have been a great inconvenience to her to have the two of us under her roof in her little house. It may have been briefly tolerable, but I did not want to inflict a distraught daughter and a teenage grandson on her. She deserved better, and besides, this move was for keeps. I needed to plan for the long term, and I was determined to stand on my own two feet for the first time in a long while. I was genuinely concerned about Mum's security and mine. Her little home was in an exposed position on a busy road that Artur would pass every day; if he saw my car there, he could track my movements, and I needed more security than that.

TEN | The battle plan

The Internet was still a fairly recent phenomenon, but I used it to my advantage to research suitable accommodation and decided on a townhouse in a suburb far enough away from the family home to feel comfortable. It had the added advantage of being closer to Tim's school but not on any direct route that Artur might use.

Most importantly the complex had secure access and onsite managers, which gave me peace of mind that there would be someone on site should we ever need help. The next day while Artur was at work, I plucked up the courage to phone the onsite managers to enquire about the unit and to arrange a viewing. The woman on the end of the phone sounded lovely, warm and professional, and I made an appointment at a time I knew would be in keeping with another of Mum's medical appointments. I asked her to come with me as this was a confronting thing to do and I needed a bit of moral support. Mum and I arrived at the complex via a long private driveway, through the electric gates after being buzzed in over the intercom system. If Artur tried to gain access to this complex, he would need to travel down the long driveway only to be turned around at the gates. Even with his inflated sense of entitlement to most things, I didn't think he'd have the balls to do that. So far, so good.

The townhouse was situated at the end of one of the streets within the complex and was quiet and private and just what Tim and I needed to begin our new life in safety. We were met by the onsite managers Joan and Jim, a lovely couple probably in their sixties, who were to become our human safety net in the weeks and months ahead. I didn't want to give too much information, but I explained that it would be just my teenage son and I moving in. Nothing was said but I knew they understood the situation, no doubt they had seen this before. A woman with a child, or children, seeking refuge in a complex where the safety features were more important than the floor space. I signed up there and then, and was just about to breathe a sigh of relief when Joan advised me that I would need to provide the usual documentation as part of the verification process. I looked quizzical and she explained "100 points proof of identification and proof of employment." I smiled back and reassured her, "I'll get them to you as soon as possible."

As I turned to leave, the smile drained from my face, and I wondered how I was going to manage to provide proof of

TEN | The battle plan

employment, as I certainly couldn't ask Artur for it. But I had to be thankful to him too, because he taught me a number of things in his cruel-to-be-kind way. Many times I had heard him say, "A problem is only a problem until it is solved." I didn't know how I was going to solve this problem, but I had no choice but to find a solution. No time to fret over it now, I had to get Mum home and then pick up Tim from the school bus to get home at my normal time. Better to sleep on it and pray for an answer.

The next day dawned and it was business as usual, so to speak. A problem shared is a problem halved, so when the opportunity presented itself, I called Maria and explained the situation to her.

"Don't worry about it," she replied, "I'll write a letter for you on company letterhead stating that you are an employee of mine. I know it's a white lie, and I normally wouldn't do something like that, but extreme circumstances call for extreme measures." I was so grateful to my dear friend, yet again, for going above and beyond the call of duty to help me when I needed it the most. I shared her unease about another white lie, but I had been unfailingly honest during my marriage and where had it got me? They say that you find out who your real friends are when you face a crisis, and I was in no doubt that I was surrounded by true and loyal friends, my sisters.

With the accommodation now sorted, I knew that I would need some furniture as I had decided not to take anything from the family home. Looking back, I'm amused by this decision. I wanted a fresh start and to surround myself with belongings that were truly mine, and not something that reminded me of the years of unhappiness I was escaping. And ridiculously, I still wanted to do the right thing! Just how conditioned was I to still want to leave an abusive marriage in a way that was as fair as possible? There would be no taking anything that wasn't mine to take. In hindsight, I wish I had been greedier, but at the time I just didn't have the stomach for it.

The benefit of living in a small townhouse is that you don't need a lot of furniture to make it feel like a home. Nevertheless, we required beds, a dining table and chairs, a sofa, a computer, a desk, and a student chair for Tim. We also needed a refrigerator, a washing machine, a clothes dryer and a microwave oven. If I was going to be working full-time, I would need these labour-saving devices, and so I went shopping! I became adept at speed shopping: whizzing into a store and making rapid decisions

TEN | The battle plan

about what I needed to buy. I only ever had a small window of opportunity to get in, do the business, and get out, so that my brief absences wouldn't be noticed. I would research everything online first; so that when I entered the store it was a very quick process to purchase what I needed in the least time possible. I arranged delayed deliveries to the new townhouse close to the date that we would be moving in.

Making these clandestine trips was nerve-wracking and I would be looking over my shoulder to see if I was being followed, fully expecting Artur to materialize unexpectedly. My heart would be thumping, and my palms would be sweaty. I just wanted to get the transaction done and get out of there. I was on tenterhooks because if I was caught now it would jeopardise everything. Thankfully my lovely, generous friends also gave me some great hand-me-down pieces that were gratefully received and proved invaluable in setting up a home on a shoestring budget.

THE GILDED CAGE

Learned Wisdom

- Unfortunately, abusive relationships don't allow for an honest and open discussion of the victim's desire to leave their partner
- Once a decision to leave the abuser has been made, tell trusted friends and family members
- Organisation and discretion are the keys to a safe and controlled exit from an abusive relationship. Delegate jobs to people you can trust – you can't do this alone

ELEVEN | The final countdown

Bit by bit I was working through the many steps required to secure my freedom, and it had become more important than ever to keep up a pretence of business as usual. In some ways I was now so emotionally removed from Artur that this was no challenge at all. I had stopped crying a long time ago. I had absolutely given up. There was no point now trying to argue my case, or to hold a mirror to the dysfunction in our marriage. My new mantra was 'the opposite of love is not hate; the opposite of love is indifference.' I had long since reached the point of indifference and it served me well, placing a protective armour around my heart.

Artur would still employ his usual tactics of goading me, insulting me, and humiliating me, but I no longer reacted. No more tear-filled attempts by me to redress the balance. No more stumbling over words and freezing, I just shrugged it all off. This had two effects: at first it was puzzling to him, and it shut down the conflict; conflict only exists where there are two willing participants. Then, realising he was getting no reaction from me, Artur doubled his efforts to belittle me. He was still trying to chip away at my self-esteem. Did I have any left?

THE GILDED CAGE

Surprisingly, making a decision to leave and putting an action plan into place had empowered me, my self-confidence was gradually returning. Being able to enlist the help of others reminded me that I was not alone, and that I was worthy of their support.

It had also taught me that nothing would change unless *I* made the change. Artur would not change his ways – he wasn't capable of it. In fact, his aggressive behaviour was still escalating: he was becoming even more antagonistic, even more unreasonable, and even more dangerous with each week that passed. I was resolute, but I was frightened, too. What if something went wrong and he stumbled onto my plan? This would be catastrophic, and it would certainly thwart any chance of a safe exit.

Knowing what was at stake, none of my beloved 'Ocean's 8' dropped the ball. Discretion was paramount, and to their credit, nobody missed a beat. It can't have been easy for them to maintain the façade, either. Any chance encounters with Artur were deftly masked with a *nothing going on here* demeanour, and telephone conversations were sometimes spoken in code just in case he was listening in.

ELEVEN | The final countdown

By now I was living on my nerves and I was bone-weary, as years of walking on eggshells had sapped my energy reserves. Ironically this also prepared me well for what was ahead. Exhaustion and fearfulness were a constant state of being, but determination and resolution are fuelled by anger, so one balanced the other. There would be no going back, I would keep going no matter what until I was free, because I had nothing left to lose.

How bad do things have to be to risk losing everything that you have? How easy is it to make a radical and irreversible change? When what you are enduring is unbearably painful and hopeless, trust me, you will risk everything and put yourself through hell to escape! When the only thing worse than losing everything is everything staying the same, it's surprising how easy the decision is. Even so, it felt like jumping across a chasm in the dark and hoping like hell that I would land safely on the other side.

Music helped me to get through the darkest days, and I would retreat to the relative safety of my car to recharge my batteries, so to speak, by listening to inspiring songs as I drove from 'a to b'. The song that resonated the most for me was 'Fighter' by

THE GILDED CAGE

Christina Aguilera. The lyrics were poignant; I felt that they had been written just for me. I would play the song over and over again when I was driving around on my own, getting stronger and more determined with each repetition. Like a boxer getting in the zone before a fight by listening to motivating tracks, this song reminded me that I was lucky to have learnt some tough lessons, and rather than breaking me down they had made me stronger than I could ever have imagined. I was not broken. I was grateful to be battle scarred, worldly wise and prepared for the combat ahead.

The lyrics still mean as much to me today, however, I am unable to reproduce them here due to copyright considerations. However, if you would like to listen to the song to understand why it was so inspiring for me, I am sure that you should be able to download it via your preferred online digital media application.

A week or so before D-Day, I picked up the keys to the townhouse; it was scary, liberating, even exhilarating, but I still had a lot of work to do before I could feel safe. Instead of detouring to the storage unit on my way to work I was now detouring to the apartment to stow the goods and chattels of my

ELEVEN | The final countdown

new life. Each day a little bit here, and a little bit there. Small items that meant the world to me: clothing, books, practical items and sentimental mementos – they were all equally important in building the next chapter in my life.

Silently, meticulously, I prepared for the day of departure. I made sure that the accounts for the business were up-to-date, the house was spotless, the washing and ironing were done, fridge and pantry stocked. I was not going to give Artur any additional fodder with which to disparage me. I'm not sure why it mattered so much to leave things in order, but I think it was a question of my dignity. I carried enough shame about not being able to make the marriage work, about making poor choices, about not being enough for him, that I didn't need the additional shame of leaving a mess behind me.

I typed a long list of instructions (would he even know where to find the iron?) for the home and the business, detailing passwords and anything that he might need in order to take responsibility for all the things I took care of. Now that I would no longer be doing what I used to do he might gain an appreciation of exactly how I filled my time! I kept the list on file on the computer and quietly added to it each time I thought of something that he would need to know. Artur had never been terribly computer-literate, and this worked in my favour. He never went near the computer, as he thought of bookkeeping as *women's work*, subtext: beneath him. So, the computer was a safe place to store my lists and other information that formed part of my escape plan. Even so, I religiously erased my browsing history and hid anything relating to the exit in misnamed files, just to be sure.

My concern about our safety at the point of departure lead me to the lowest point of my journey, quietly sobbing at the local police station. With only days now until we would be leaving, the final countdown had begun. There was still so much to do, I was already exhausted, and I was miserable with a cold. There were moments when I felt so low that I didn't think I would make it; I just couldn't see how I would get everything done in time. But curiously, when I had those moments, a little voice in my head would say, "This is only for a few more days, keep going no matter what, you can rest on the other side." And so, I would continue on, because no matter how hard it was to keep working on leaving, it would be a whole lot harder to stay.

ELEVEN | The final countdown

Learned Wisdom

- Don't be tempted to give up your plans if things become difficult. Remember, where domestic violence exists nothing will change unless *you* change
- While 'white collar' abusers don't usually resort to physical violence, any change in circumstances could change their *modus operandi*
- Notify the police in advance of your intention to leave so that they can be aware of your personal safety concerns
- The more preparation you do and the more organised you are the more successful and safer your exit will be
- Try to take the emotion out of the equation, remember it is a process just like any other

TWELVE | Exodus

Leaving day arrived, the last Friday of the term, the start of a three-week school break. It was all a little surreal, going through the motions of life as usual: have breakfast, get ready for the day, stick to the ritual of having a cup of coffee with Artur at the nearby café just before starting work. ***Don't make any changes just yet, stick to the script, just for one more day.*** Work was a bit of a blur that day, I think I did a convincing job of behaving normally, but it's hard to be sure, impossible to be objective about it, as I had no perspective away from ground zero. However, I had years of experience in putting on a good front to others, so really this was my usual way of operating, just with a bit more at stake this time.

The hardest part was not being able to say goodbye to our lovely staff members, regular customers and other store holders in the shopping centre. I had formed friendships and friendly acquaintances with many of them, and it hurt me to think that I wouldn't be able to give them the courtesy of saying goodbye, let alone an explanation for my sudden departure. It just couldn't be done. I couldn't dwell on what people might think of me for what I was doing. My safety, and my son's safety, overrode any need to account for my actions. There would be no going back, I didn't even want to step foot in the building again if it could be avoided.

When my shift finished it was time to bank the takings from the previous day, and while waiting in the queue I had one of many **'well this is the last time I'll be doing this'** moments. Yes, of course I banked the money into the business account, it certainly never occurred to me to hang on to it. It would have been stealing, and wasn't that what Artur had been doing over the years: skimming off money from the shop for his own benefit? Now wasn't the time for me to start behaving the same way.

After doing the banking and running the usual errands for work and home, I picked up Tim from the bus and we headed home for the last time. The three of us had an early dinner as usual so that Artur could do the 5pm to 9pm shift at the sweet shop. I was trying to appear *normal*, but my heart was beating faster than usual, and it was getting harder and harder not to be jumpy. *Any minute now, any minute now.*

TWELVE | Exodus

When Artur left for work, he was not his usual self, his mood was brooding and ominous, as though he suspected that this was not going to be an evening like any other. Had he become aware of something not being quite normal? I'll never know for sure, but his behaviour was unsettling: he was disturbingly quiet and acted with an intensity that normally preceded his awful outbursts.

He knows. Oh, dear God, I think he knows! Artur was standing in the doorway, looking back at me before he left for work. I saw an expression on his face that I had never seen before. I have seen malice, I have seen contempt, I have seen disgust, but this was new, it was intense, and it burned right through me. My heart was thumping in my chest, yet I kept up the pretence as I was conditioned to do, with a neutral look on my face. *Nothing going on here.* His stare lasted for what seemed like an eternity, and finally he turned and walked out of the door. It was time for me to go too, but I wouldn't be coming back.

I picked up my phone and called Eileen. She had been on standby nearby, and I gave her the all-clear to come and help us with the last-minute packing. When I wrote earlier that I would not take any furniture, there was one exception, and that was the formal lounge suite. For some reason I had formed an emotional attachment to it, and I wanted to take it with me; after all, it was used infrequently and would hardly be missed. I had owned it for many years before we got married, and I loved it as a beautiful piece of furniture. I had chosen the style and fabric and had (impatiently) waited for weeks for it to be custom made. My delight when the three-seat sofa and two armchairs were finally delivered was childlike, and over the years I never tired of its presence or the comfort it provided. Eileen had organised a man-with-a-small-truck to arrive with her so that we could pile the lounge suite on to it and take it with us. It wasn't easy as the pieces were very well made, what I really mean by that is that it was heavy! But between the driver, Eileen, Tim and I we managed it. The next hour or so was a blur of frantic eleventh-hour packing, of throwing things into bags and loading up my car and Eileen's car.

To my great shame, I can remember at one point shouting at Tim who was having trouble deciding over items to pack. The look of shock on his face was heart breaking, and it has stayed with me ever since. It was rare for me to raise my voice and he was justifiably shocked. I felt wretched for shouting at him; this must have been a confusing and frightening time for him too. I

TWELVE | Exodus

reassured him that he would be able to take whatever he needed, and I realised then I had to calm down and take a few deep breaths.

Unsurprisingly I had made a checklist of the last-minute items to pack and the tasks to do to make sure that nothing was missed, that nothing was left behind. I had already downloaded all my files, including the business and accounting files onto discs, as there were no USB sticks back then. I deleted the browsing history and anything else on the computer that might provide information about our new whereabouts.

I left a letter propped on the kitchen bench where Artur would find it when he came home from work. I had taken my time writing the letter in stolen moments in the days prior, choosing my words carefully. I wanted him to fully understand my reasons for leaving and for there to be no ambiguity whatsoever that Tim and I would not be returning. It was not a harsh letter, it was considered and clear and firm, but it was not spiteful. The envelope also contained all the instructions, information and passwords that Artur would need to continue on without me. It would be my last letter, and I had a faint hope it would be read in the spirit with which it was written.

THE GILDED CAGE

I then grabbed the address book that always sat on the kitchen benchtop near the home phone and popped it into my handbag for safekeeping. While we had mobile phones, this was long before the days of smart phones. Details of our contacts were stored in a hard copy address book kept handy near the home phone. This was no random act, my intention was to protect my friends, especially those who had facilitated the break. Without their contact details, Artur would be unable to approach them or harass them, at least not without showing his hand.

A last check through all the rooms and we were out of the door. The Gilded Cage had lost its lustre and shone no more, the hinges on the door had corroded over time and the door gave way easily as the bird pushed against it, free at last and never to return. Exodus!

Out into the fresh air, and my heart was pounding but I was barely breathing, adrenaline coursing through my veins at a million miles per hour. Artur had behaved so strangely when he left for work; would he just suddenly appear and put an end to all this? Out on the street he was nowhere to be seen, so with one final look back towards the house I started the car and our odd little convoy of cars – me with Tim, Eileen, and the-man-

TWELVE | Exodus

with-a-small-truck – made our way slowly and surely to the townhouse. It was a trip of less than half an hour, but it felt like the journey of a lifetime. All I wanted was to make it through the gates of the complex and be safely tucked away in our new little home.

When our convoy arrived, my Mum was there to greet us. I had arranged for a taxi to take her to the townhouse earlier in the day, so she could have a few things ready for our arrival. After lugging the sofa and chairs (which by now seemed to be getting larger and heavier each time we handled them) off the truck and into the living room, we farewelled the driver and quickly unpacked the items from Eileen's car. She was only able to stay briefly because she was still 'keeping the secret' so unpacking her car was a priority. A quick hug and she drove home. I parked my car in the garage and shut the roller door and then Tim, Mum and I dragged the remaining items from my car into the townhouse and dumped them in the middle of the floor. The stress of the last few hours, let alone the last few days, had evidently taken its toll. We were all drained and needed a moment or two to reflect and recharge, so we took time out for a cup of tea, Mum's panacea for all worries. We sat quietly drinking our tea, tired, numb and trying to process the bizarre events of the last few hours.

After some unpacking and a light supper, we headed upstairs to make up our beds and to sleep; bone weary and heavy headed. Lights off, there would be time for more unpacking and settling- in tomorrow. I lay awake for some time, hoping for sleep to find me but it was evasive. In the dark my mind started to race, this room was unfamiliar, I felt vulnerable and foolish. What had I just done? I must be mad!! Cold terror gripped me. Just who did I think I was to leave my home and my husband? How on earth would I survive? I know, I would call him in the morning and explain it was all a mistake and Tim and I would go back to Artur and all would be well. Then, as I had done too many times during my marriage, I quietly cried myself to sleep.

TWELVE | Exodus

Learned Wisdom

- Summon up all your courage and self-control to stay calm on 'exit day'. You are nearly there!
- Use last-minute checklists to make sure you do everything you need to do in the right order as you leave: you will only get one chance to make a safe, clean exit
- Be prepared to experience a range of emotions at the point of leaving and in the days following

THIRTEEN | A new order

The next morning I woke to the sound of birdsong. The sun had not fully risen, and I lay there in the pre-dawn darkness contemplating the events of the previous day. All was quiet, no one else was stirring in the townhouse, so there was no immediate need to get out of bed. Perhaps it had been exhaustion that fuelled my panic the previous evening, and maybe a good night's sleep was all that was needed to restore my resolve. No, I would not go back now, I had come this far, I would keep moving forward. I knew there would be good days and not-so-good days ahead, but I felt stronger than I had in a long time and surely nothing in the future could be any worse than I had endured during my marriage. This was the beginning of a New Order.

After breakfast, Mum and I finished off the last of the unpacking, while Tim commenced the unenviable task of constructing the flat pack furniture. A desk, a bookcase, a table and dining chairs were no small feat for a first timer. Mum and I helped by holding the pieces in place while he plied the Allen key or the electric drill driver. Buying flat pack pieces (and some gratefully received hand-me-downs) had been the only way I could afford to furnish our new little home. The pre-emptive purchase of a modestly priced electric drill driver proved to be a wise investment, Tim was quite a wiz with it, and had the pieces put together in no time at all. What an amazing young man he was! I couldn't have been more proud of him. He got on with the job with quiet dignity and determination and never complained once about having to move to a much smaller home or having to wrangle an Allen key or a drill bit.

I was painfully aware that I was moving Tim away from all that was familiar to him, but especially from his best friend who lived in the same street. However, I was determined that everything else would remain the same: same school, same local footy club where he had played each season since the under nines, and same friends. Apart from not living in a large unhappy home, all else would be unchanged. There were three weeks of school holidays ahead of us, it would be enough time to get settled in and to form new routines. Our own new sense of normal before school resumed.

But there was one piece of business I had to attend to first. Artur had rung my mobile phone the previous evening and I ignored

THIRTEEN | A new order

the call as I was in no state to talk to him. I sat staring at the phone and my stomach churned when I saw his name flash up on the screen. I couldn't withstand another of his invectives, not now. Then it occurred to me that I didn't have to accept his call just yet. I had spent 14 years dancing to his tune, and I had earned the right to choose when to speak to him. Naturally he left a voicemail, but I couldn't bring myself to listen to it then and there. I promised myself that I would do him the courtesy of calling him back, but only when I had the strength to. But now this was a brand-new day and I knew I couldn't delay talking to Artur indefinitely. It would keep gnawing at me until I faced the music, so it was better to get it out of the way than to let it fester.

First things first, I sat at the top of the stairs, took a deep breath, closed my eyes, and listened to the message. Artur spoke slowly and deliberately in a calculated fashion, and it was unnerving to listen to. He acknowledged that I needed space, but in his opinion Tim and I should return home as soon as possible. Clearly this was some phase I was going through and when I came to my senses, I would realise that our rightful place was back in the family home as one happy unit. Hmm. And there it was in a nutshell: if Tim and I returned home before too much damage was done, he would forgive me! Let me translate that for you: "If you come home before anyone finds out that my wife and son have left me, I will save myself from embarrassment." I figured that there was no time like the present, so I called his number and he picked up immediately. We only talked for a few minutes, but his message was clear: come back home now and you will be forgiven. My message was equally as clear: what part of "not coming back" don't you understand? At first it was a calm and adult conversation, but as it dawned on him that I really was not coming back he became his old self, vengeful and spiteful. If I had needed any validation that I had done the right thing, there it was in that phone call. I managed to get a few words in, and I agreed with him that we would need to talk again about future arrangements. Yes, Tim and I were safe and sound, and no he didn't need to know where we were. That first phone call after leaving the family home was challenging, but it was a watershed moment. For the first time I was able to clearly articulate to Artur that our marriage was over.

The following day I received a phone call from the local police, saying that they were at the gate and they wanted to come and talk to me. I buzzed them into the complex thinking *this is a*

THIRTEEN | A new order

good look, I only moved in two days ago and the police are already calling on me. Disregarding what my new neighbours might be thinking of me I welcomed two uniformed police officers through the door. They explained they were doing a welfare check to see how I was settling in and to find out if Artur had tried to contact me. This was incredibly decent of them, as I now lived outside their police district, and they had come out of their way to see me. Mum sat with me as we explained that all had been well, that I had had no physical contact with Artur, and that we three were doing fine. The officers advised me that they had attended the family home on the night Tim and I left and had removed a number of unregistered firearms from the premises. Naturally they were not at liberty to tell me more except that Artur had been displeased with this turn of events.

For a man who, for the most part, considered himself above the law this would have been difficult for Artur to stomach. The penalties for possessing unregistered firearms in Australia are severe, so Artur should have considered himself lucky not to be prosecuted for the offence. Perhaps the police were concerned that his indignation would drive him to exact some retribution on me. For now, at least, I was confident Artur was not aware

THE GILDED CAGE

of my whereabouts and he knew he was now on his local police station's radar.

Now that the dust had settled, it was time for me to make a few phone calls to tell those friends, who had not been part of my inner circle, what had happened, and that Tim and I were fine. One of my first calls was to Katie, the mother of Tim's best friend Noah. She was relieved to hear from me as she said she guessed something wasn't quite right. She continued to explain that Noah had called over to the family home the day after we left to see if Tim wanted to go to their house to play video games. Artur had answered the door and replied that Tim would not be able to see Noah as he and I had gone away on holiday. Katie said she knew that wasn't right, as Tim and I would never be allowed to have a break away on our own. I pretended not to be bothered by this, but it was a sobering moment, to think that even the neighbours could tell that we wouldn't have permission to have time away from Artur.

Katie and I were neighbours more than we were friends, and although she had my old home phone number, she didn't have my mobile number. She had been unable to contact me directly to find out what was going on. I invited Noah and Katie to visit

THIRTEEN | A new order

us, as it would be good for Tim to have his best friend by his side now. Katie fully understood the need for privacy and agreed not to share any of our information with Artur. She was a steadfast, strong and fiercely intelligent woman and though neither she nor I knew it then, she would safeguard my independence.

It was a joyous moment when Katie and Noah arrived at our new home. They were our first guests and it was just the tonic Tim and I needed. The boys settled in together as though nothing of any importance had occurred in the last 48 hours, they didn't miss a beat! This was the reassurance that I was looking for in measuring how Tim was really coping with our change in circumstances. Looking at how contented he was hanging out with his best friend was encouraging. Katie, Mum and I decided to have morning tea outside in the little back garden. Because our unit was an end-of-terrace, we had some additional outdoor space, a delightful little garden to the back and rear of the town house, fully fenced and very safe. The complex also backed on to a reserve along a natural waterway and there was plenty of open space and green grass for Tim and his mates to stretch out and play footy or ride their bikes. As we settled in to our morning tea, the boys grabbed a couple of biscuits each and a football and headed out to the green space to kick the ball around.

When the boys had left Katie enquired, "What about work, what are your plans there?" She knew that I worked in the family business and rightly assumed that I wouldn't be working there again.

"Well, I'll be actively looking as soon as school resumes. For now, I have enough to get by on and I just want to be here for Tim for the next few weeks. But I'll absolutely have to work full time to make ends meet," I replied.

I made it sound so matter-of-fact, but to be honest I was a little more than confronted by the thought of job hunting when I had worked in the family business in one way or another for so long. But what the hell, I no longer had a comfort zone, every day now was a new adventure and every day scared me and thrilled me all at once. *Better strap in and hang on for the ride!* Katie and I chatted for a while longer until it was time for her and Noah to leave. The boys were enjoying themselves so much that we had trouble dragging them away from their game. *What a great problem to have*, I thought.

THIRTEEN | A new order

As Katie and Noah left, I stood at the front door of my new home and reflected that I was not at all embarrassed by my reduced circumstances, far from it. Sure, Katie, her husband and their children lived in a large home, most of the houses in our old street were large executive-style homes. But I was really proud of my new space, it was safe, it was comfortable and tidy, and it had everything we truly needed. Most of all it was free from controlling behaviour and sadness and fear, and I couldn't put a price on that.

There was still more post-exit *housekeeping* to do, and it was wonderful to have Mum on hand to help out while I attended to a long to-do list. She would return home once the dust had settled and I could be sure that Artur would not turn up on her doorstep. One of the first phone calls I made was to the Department of Foreign Affairs and Trade (DEFAT) to request a Child Alert be placed on Tim's passport. A Child Alert is a warning to DEFAT that there may be circumstances to be considered before an Australian passport is issued to a child. Even though Tim had his own passport, I believed it was not beyond Artur to report it as stolen and request a replacement passport. In the early days post separation, I was fearful that Artur might try to take Tim back to the 'old country' and that

THE GILDED CAGE

he would never be seen again. There were forms to complete and lodge, and certain criteria to meet, but with the police having been involved this was easily done.

Next on the list was to phone Tim's school to advise them of the change in our circumstances. Even though it was the school holidays I knew that some administrative staff would be on hand, and they could not have been more professional or helpful. Sadly, circumstances like mine were not unheard of, and they had procedures in place for these situations. Until advised otherwise, Tim was not to be collected from school by his father, and both parents would receive copies of all correspondence from the school. Additionally, my lawyer wrote to the headmaster confirming the change in circumstances for Tim and me, and instructing the school not to release our new address to Artur, or anyone else, without my consent.

I also applied successfully to the Electoral Office for a 'silent registration' so that my address could not be published or divulged without my consent. And finally, I did the same for my driver's licence so that Artur could not ascertain my whereabouts through the transport department. It amounted to

THIRTEEN | A new order

a fair amount of time, phone calls and form-filling, but it was worth every effort taken to give me the peace of mind I needed.

Club footy took a break during the school holidays, so I rang Tim's team coach to advise him of the change in our circumstances, just so he could keep an eye on Tim should Artur uncharacteristically turn up to training or a match when footy resumed. It was during my conversation with the coach that I realised that Artur had never taken Tim to footy training. In fairness to Artur he worked most night shifts and couldn't reasonably be expected to fit in Tim's twice weekly training sessions. It didn't, however, excuse him for rarely attending Tim's weekend footy games. Artur always had some justification, especially if it was an away game. Eventually our disappointment at Artur not being at the games gave way to relief. Without him, Tim and I could relax a little and wouldn't have to walk on eggshells.

When club footy resumed it was heartening to see how the families rallied around Tim and I. Doubtless the word had spread, and his teammates and their families were somewhat protective of us. Maybe my years of volunteering in the canteen for Friday night training and home game days stood me in good stead. I had always figured that while I was at the clubhouse for training or a home game I might as well make myself useful and give a hand in the canteen with some of the other mums. That is, of course, other than when Tim's team was playing, because then I would be on the sidelines with all the other parents cheering our boys on. The exception to this was Artur, and some parents asked me how they would recognise him if he turned up, as they had never met him. Enough said.

THIRTEEN | A new order

Learned wisdom

- Make contact with your ex-partner only when you feel strong enough to, but be reasonable about the time frame if there are children involved
- The first conversation with your ex-partner (whether it is via text, telephone, or in person) won't be easy, but you should experience some sense of relief afterwards
- Contact any friends or family members who have not been privy to your exit plans as soon as possible
- Be honest with them about your reasons for leaving and any concerns you have for your personal safety
- White-collar abuse is easy to hide from yourself, your family, and your friends. The time for covering it up has passed, it's time for honesty and openness from here on
- Be mindful of your social media exposure, review your security settings and think very carefully about any activity here
- Notify all relevant authorities and government agencies about your change in circumstances as soon as possible. Apply for restricted access to your personal details or

silent registrations where possible if you have concerns for your personal safety

FOURTEEN | Back to business

Before I could get too comfortable with my new Artur-free life, he requested a face-to-face meeting with Tim and me. In some ways this wasn't unreasonable, I could understand that he might want to see Tim in person to make sure that he really was okay. On the other hand, I knew Artur of old and he would be using all his manipulative skills to unsettle me, so I might again consider reconciling with him. I was not prepared to meet him alone, so I arranged the use of a meeting room at the lawyer's office. The walls were made of glass so that everything would be quite literally transparent, and my lawyer offered to sit in with us initially to get a sense of Artur's intention for the meeting. I had Mum with me too for moral support, but that didn't stop my stomach churning with dread.

Those first few minutes felt about as awkward as a really bad first date, and in some ways that's what it was. This was uncharted territory for us all and everyone was searching for his or her place in it. Artur tried to engage with Tim, and to Tim's credit he was polite, but he was not returning the interest. Artur announced that he wanted to be able to spend some time with Tim on a regular basis, but he was not seeking any formal custody (or residency, as it was then known) arrangement. This was prior to the introduction of the 2006 changes to the Australian *Family Law Act* where the presumption was that the child, or children, would reside 50-50 with each parent, as the starting point. Given Tim's age, his wishes would be considered in any formal residency order handed down from the Family Court and surely deep-down Artur knew that Tim did not want to live with him. Equally, I didn't believe for one minute that Artur would want to have the responsibility for fulltime care of Tim, but this was his chance to put it on the table if he did want it. And he didn't.

We touched on future financial arrangements and Artur announced that he would pay for Tim's school fees but not a cent for anything else. I certainly wasn't seeking spousal support, the last thing I wanted was financial dependence on a man I had little respect for, but I did expect him to share the financial obligation for caring for his son. His pronouncement illustrated how little he understood about the true costs of raising a child. Don't misunderstand me, I was grateful for Artur's assurance to cover the school fees, because keeping Tim at the same school was essential to maintaining as much

FOURTEEN | Back to business

consistency for him as possible. However, Artur's stance fell far short of contributing to provide shelter, food and clothing for a growing boy, or the cost of schoolbooks, uniforms, sporting fees and equipment, music tuition and so on. Having said that, this came as no surprise for me because I knew this man better than he knew himself. Of course, he would not offer to pay his fair share of the costs of raising his son, he had begrudgingly contributed while we were married so why would he change now?

Artur was watching me closely to see if he had ruffled my feathers with this last salvo, but I shrugged and said, "All of this can be fine-tuned in due course." Years of living under his control had prepared me well for how he would behave, and he was proving to be as predictable and as regular as clockwork. The meeting ended with an understanding that we would continue with an informal and self-managed arrangement regarding residency and time shared with each parent, with consideration given to Tim's wishes. But meeting the financial obligation for Tim's needs remained unresolved and I could tell it was going to have to be fought tooth and nail.

THE GILDED CAGE

Soon enough the school term started, and it was back to the real world, so to speak. Mum had returned safely to her home, and under the gaze of the local police service, Artur had not dared to darken her doorway. Tim settled back into school life and I was grateful that we both had the routine of the school day, the commute, training sessions for school and club sports, and homework to give us a sense of everything being back to normal.

Now it was time for me to focus on getting a job so that we could sustain our newfound freedom. A few weeks had passed since leaving and my modest bank balance was dwindling ever so surely. At this rate I'd be out of money before too long and that would be disastrous on all fronts; it was time to get back to business.

The first item on my get-a-job plan (yes, old habits die hard and I had made a list of what I thought I needed to do to find suitable employment) was to update my resumé. It quite literally needed dusting off and revising. It didn't take too long to put a draft together and soon I had the semblance of a half-decent resumé to shop around. I had just finished admiring my handiwork when my phone rang, and it was my friend Cathy

FOURTEEN | Back to business

calling. Her son Marcus was in the same year at Tim's school, and as they lived nearby the boys often travelled to school together. Cathy and her husband Ian were lovely folks, a great couple and the sort of people who restored my faith in the institution of marriage. They were devoted parents to their two boys, active in school life and thoroughly decent souls. Their friendship was something I cherished, and I was grateful that I hadn't lost them in the fallout.

Cathy was phoning to see how I was going and to see if I would like to catch up for coffee. I invited her over as she hadn't been to the townhouse yet, and during the course of our chat I showed her the draft of my updated resumé. She read through it and in the kindest way possible she ventured, "You know Ian is a graphic artist, don't you?" I nodded, Cathy's husband Ian was a designer of some renown and had been responsible for creating some very well-known marketing campaigns and logos. I could see where Cathy was heading with this, redesigning my humble resumé would be a walk in the park for Ian. She volunteered his services and I immediately accepted her generous offer.

THE GILDED CAGE

I emailed Cathy a copy of my resumé for Ian to work on and left the rest up to him. Even though I was proud of my new resumé, I knew a professional touch would really make the difference to how effective it could be. It seemed as though the universe was looking after me by sending me the very people I needed at exactly the right time.

After my coffee date with Cathy I pondered on how few of my friends I had lost as collateral damage in the aftermath of my marriage breakdown. They say that you find out who your real friends are in times of crisis, and I was discovering how true this was. I expected some attrition after walking away from Artur, but I was pleasantly surprised to find how many of our friends stuck by me. I don't just mean that they kept in contact; these people were going all-out to assist Tim and I in real and meaningful ways. When I thought about it further, it struck me that many of *our* friends had been *my* friends. I had been the one valuing and nurturing the friendships, remembering birthdays and anniversaries, keeping in touch and being genuinely interested in their wellbeing. **Do unto others, as you would have them do unto you.**

FOURTEEN | Back to business

Learned Wisdom

- Make sure any face-to-face meetings with your ex-partner are well managed. Consider meeting in 'neutral territory' and never meet alone. I would always meet the image-conscious Artur in public places, knowing that he would not behave poorly in front of an audience
- Now is the time to focus on the future, try not to dwell on the past, the past is gone
- Accept help when it is offered, even if it is from unexpected sources. Allowing someone to assist you is an act of strength

FIFTEEN | Opportunity knocks

What goes up must come down, and my happiness at starting over a new life, and my optimism for the future, was quickly dissolving. I had been running on adrenaline for weeks, months really, but now I was falling in a heap. No longer did I wake up feeling full of enthusiasm for the day ahead, rather I woke up feeling scared and desperate. Anxiety would have been the more accurate description but using the correct terminology didn't make me feel any better about it.

I could manage everything else: no longer being in the family home, losing my marriage, having no money. But having no job was harder to bear. It had always been a source of personal pride that I had worked hard outside the home and contributed to the family income, no matter how small that may have been. Being unemployed was something I had not dealt with before, but now I understood what people meant when they said that it is the pride in working that is as important as the paycheque. I had a new perspective and genuine empathy for people who were involuntarily without work.

THE GILDED CAGE

I did my best to hide my deteriorating mental state from Tim, he certainly didn't need know that his mother was struggling to keep it all together. So, I confided my distress to Tina, as she was a safe sounding board, a woman who understood how fragile mental health could be. She reassured me that my anxiety was understandable and was probably a healthy response to the events of the past few months. While it was great to have her understanding it still didn't make me feel any better about myself.

Then I did what I probably should have done weeks earlier and booked an appointment with my doctor. I sobbed through my consultation as I explained the events that had led me there and she reassured me that my anxiety and depression was a reasonable response to the strain I had been under for years. She prescribed me some antidepressants and I took them willingly because I desperately wanted to feel happier and stronger than I felt in that moment. So, I did what I could, I just kept on keeping on. Soon I would have my resumé and then I would pull out all the stops to get myself a job.

In the meantime, there were the daily and the weekly routines to help keep my mind off myself and my concern for my

FIFTEEN | Opportunity knocks

dwindling cash reserves. The commencement of the school term had heralded the resumption of club footy and this week the game was at the home ground. I was pleased to catch up with all the other footy mums; it was another indication that life was getting back to normal. Katie was sitting on one of the benches in anticipation of our boys' game starting, she waved me over and I sat down next to her. We chatted about things in general for a few minutes and then she turned to me and said, "I'm helping to set up a new department at work and I'm looking for someone who can help me with administrative duties, but to start with it would be answering the phone to handle enquiries. Would you be interested?" I couldn't believe my ears, I was being offered a job that I was sure I could do, and it didn't involve standing on my feet all day.

What's that sound? Oh, it's not an alarm bell, this time it's opportunity knocking!

"That sounds wonderful, of course I'd be interested," I managed to reply calmly. Even though I was jumping up and down on the inside I held it together because I wanted to behave professionally, there was no need to make Katie regret her offer already. Katie went on to explain that she needed someone who could start immediately (no problem there!), who could work full-time hours, and who had experience in office administration and marketing. To be honest, if she had offered me a job cleaning the toilets, I would have jumped at it, but this was so much more. She said she would phone me in a week or so to discuss it further, but for now she was pleased to know that I was interested in the role.

And there it was, the universe was stepping in again to help me when I needed it the most. What had just happened? That was the most curious job interview I had ever had. If I did get the job, it would secure our future; and if I didn't get the job at least I had learned that someone had considered me employable. I decided not to focus on it in the meantime, as I was still managing to keep busy attending to the many tasks that I didn't anticipate after rearranging my life.

For instance, I had made the decision to return to my maiden name because I felt that I needed a new sense of identity and that my husband's surname had no place in my new life. It was a liberating experience and it really did help me to forge a newfound individuality. I was no longer half of a couple. I was equal to a 'whole' on my own.

FIFTEEN | Opportunity knocks

I discovered that in most instances to change my name on official documents the application needed to be made in person, not online. I couldn't change my name on my driver licence until I had some documentation with my new (old) name on it. So, I went to Medicare first to update my name there, and then I could use my new Medicare card and my birth certificate to update my driver licence, bank account, electoral roll entry, passport, Australian Tax Office profile, and so on.

Back then it was a laborious and time-consuming task, but these days Medicare offers a fee-for-service facility that assists people to change their name with other government organisations as well, quickly and conveniently. I wish this had been available to me then as I had a real sense of urgency about getting my house in order. I knew that I wouldn't have the time to attend to the minutiae of personal housekeeping once I was working full time.

A few days later, I received the call from Katie that I had been waiting on, I hardly dared to breathe as she spoke, "I'm just phoning to say that the approval has been given and the job's yours, if you are still interested".

THE GILDED CAGE

I couldn't get the words out quickly enough, "Yes, I'm definitely interested, I'd be delighted to accept the position." We talked for a few minutes more about the hours, what the specific requirements of the job were, my pay level and that I would start the following week. Katie apologised that the rate of pay wasn't higher, but little did she know that it was double what I had earned working in the family business. I assured her that the amount offered was perfectly fine and that I couldn't wait to start. This job offer was ideal, the salary would be more than enough to survive on, it would cover the rent and all living expenses, additional expenses for Tim's education, legal expenses and maybe leave a little over for a future fund. Almost immediately my anxiety lifted, and I could see the light at the end of the tunnel, and it wasn't an oncoming train!

That weekend, I did something I had wanted to do for a long time, but hadn't been able to manage until now. I grabbed Tim and took him to the local bike shop and bought him a new bike. He had already outgrown his old bike, but it just hadn't been possible to buy a new one with so much financial uncertainty hanging over my head. Now I could easily justify the expense and take comfort in not seeing my boy riding around on his bike

FIFTEEN | Opportunity knocks

with his knees up around his chin. We were going to be fine, somehow, I just knew it.

When the universe decides to throw some luck your way, it often happens in multiples. Cathy phoned to say that Ian had finished my resumé and that he would email me a pdf version, and a Word version in case I needed to update it at any time in the future. Even though I had a job now and technically didn't need my new resumé, I was still very grateful to Cathy and Ian for helping me with it. I didn't mention to Cathy that I already had a job lined up, but I felt that they had been partly responsible for my good fortune any way. I figured that the universe could see that I was ready for a new start and that I was prepared to work hard for it and that preparing my new resumé had been an act of good faith on my behalf.

Ian had done an outstanding job on my resumé, it was far more professional and visually appealing than anything I could have produced, even with my writing and marketing experience. I valued my new resumé for what it represented and took it with me on my first day at my new job.

I handed it to Katie and said, "You should probably know more about my professional background, so this might help you to get to know me better." I had to ask the question that had been gnawing at me, and there was no time like the present, so I ventured, "Can I ask why you offered me the job? We haven't worked together before and I must be a bit of an unknown quantity." Katie smiled and motioned for me to sit, she looked me directly in the eye and said, "Well, I watched you organise our street parties, how you volunteered at the club football canteen, and how you ran your business. Remember we were customers there more than once. You clearly have customer service skills, administrative abilities and you are organised. Besides, I know that you really need this job, so it's clear to me that you'll do your best and that's all I ask."

I had been starved for years of hearing anything resembling a compliment, so Katie's words touched me deeply. I was astonished to learn that something as humble as organising the Christmas street parties in our cul-de-sac or volunteering in a canteen would leave a positive impression on someone. Or that one day it would lead to a life-enhancing job offer. It just goes to show that you are always being observed and you are judged on your behaviours more than your words. Hard work and good intent can lead to rewards never imagined.

FIFTEEN | Opportunity knocks

I loved my new role; it allowed me to stretch my wings for the first time in a very long while. I relished the challenge of working in a new environment and a new field, and I valued the respectful culture within the department, and the esteem in which the parent organisation was held. It made me proud to say I worked for them, and I worked damn hard at doing my very best professionally and personally.

There was time now to take stock of where I was, how I was travelling and what my next priority should be. Tim and I were secure in our new home, it continued to provide us with comfort and a safe roof over our heads, as onsite managers Joan and Jim were keeping a more than proprietary eye on us. Tim had settled back into school life and the routine of schoolwork, homework, training and sporting fixtures were keeping him nicely busy. I had secure employment and a steady income, and I was gaining newfound confidence in my abilities and a renewed sense of self-worth every day. So, what next? It was time to face up to Artur and bring him to account for the years of abuse he had gotten away with.

It was time to seek a financial settlement.

THE GILDED CAGE

Learned Wisdom

- Be prepared for dips in your emotional wellbeing. Escaping abuse and forging a new life is a huge undertaking
- If you feel that your mental health is suffering, speak up and get help. The sooner you do this, the sooner you will feel better
- You will be faced with many new experiences, don't be overwhelmed by them, embrace them. You won't make any progress staying in your comfort zone
- When opportunity knocks, open the door!

PART THREE

SIXTEEN | Survival of the organised

There are three elements to address when a marriage or a relationship ends. If there are any children from the relationship, the foremost issue is parenting and the future care of the children. The second consideration is negotiating a financial settlement between the two parties. And, if the two parties were married, the third consideration is a formal dissolution of the marriage, or divorce. Artur had indicated that he did not want any formal parenting arrangement and I had to take him at his word, unless I was otherwise advised. Although I knew that I would seek a divorce, the statutory 12-month separation period needed to be observed, so that could wait for now.

The time had finally come to hold Artur to account. In simple terms, this meant seeking *Financial Orders* through the Family Law Court, where a decision would be made on the division (distribution) of our property and financial assets. And for most intents and purposes the orders would finalise the financial relationship between Artur and me.

THE GILDED CAGE

I made an appointment with my lawyer with the purpose of taking the first steps towards a financial settlement. Artur had already indicated to me that there was no need for a financial settlement because any property or financial assets *we* owned were clearly *his* alone. I was exasperated, yet unsurprised, by his pronouncement. Of course, after fourteen years as a faithful, devoted and loving wife, I would be entitled to nothing! I'm sure he was genuinely surprised that I would have the audacity to instigate a financial claim from him. After all, from his perspective he had brought all the wealth to the marriage. End of. Evidently all the years I worked long hours for little pay for the family businesses counted for nothing.

It amused me that I was not fit to be a beneficiary of any assets or wealth, but I had been mighty useful in co-signing loan documents when he needed me to. My lawyer was already aware of the unusual arrangement of the third-party ownership of the family home, and that I was not a named beneficiary. It would take some work to untangle that, to prove that Artur and I were the rightful owners of the property, and that the third-party trust existed only so he could hide assets. My lawyer asked me a long list of questions while trying to gain a clearer picture of the financial landscape of our marriage. I answered

SIXTEEN | Survival of the organised

truthfully and in as much detail as I could because I knew that his advocacy on my behalf would only be as effective as the information I gave him.

There were some questions he asked, to which I didn't have the answers at hand. I wrote a list of the information he needed and assured him I would provide him with the facts as soon as possible.

My lawyer continued on to outline the process for seeking *Financial Orders* and explained that there was a schedule of steps, or protocols, that needed to be undertaken in a specific order. In ideal circumstances the two parties would reach their own agreement on how the assets of the marriage would be shared, and providing it met certain criteria, the court would uphold their agreement. Coming from an environment where financial abuse was the default operating system, it was unlikely I could take this preferred pathway. I knew I would have to fight long and hard for any concession from Artur, and as I outlined how the finances had been managed between us my lawyer was coming to this realisation as well.

It was explained to me that the general principles for a court to settle financial disputes, under the Australian *Family Law Act*

1975, are based on: identifying the assets and liabilities and determining their worth; considering the financial and non-financial contributions of both parties during the marriage; and the future needs of any children.

The first step was for me to provide the basic information requested by my lawyer: dates, places, personal and financial details and so on. Back home, I got to work and typed a clear response via email. I set out each question in dot point format with the answer or relevant information following, using indented dot points where necessary. I knew that it was vital to set out the information clearly and concisely and to stick to the facts. I read my response through twice and made amendments until I was satisfied that it addressed all the issues raised by my lawyer, then sent the email immediately.

This was a process that would be followed repeatedly over the coming weeks and months and I assumed that the information was coming together nicely, so that my lawyer had a very clear picture of what the specific issues of the case were. Naturally I would be sent an invoice each month for work undertaken on my behalf, and the charges were considerable to say the least.

SIXTEEN | Survival of the organised

Somehow, I managed to keep up to date with them, but it stretched my finances to the limit.

Artur had decided to self-represent and his decision made me raise an eyebrow. Considering that English was his second language, I thought this would put him at a disadvantage. He had a close friend who was a lawyer, surely he would have stepped in to represent Artur, or at least recommended someone else? I believed that it was an indication of Artur's arrogance and ignorance that he thought that he could self-represent in this circumstance. He was certain that I had no right to any claim, and he thought so little of it that he deemed it unworthy of engaging a lawyer. Oh well, it was his decision.

As the weeks turned into months, I became increasingly frustrated by the lack of attention to detail shown by my lawyer.

Documents sent to me for checking before they would be submitted to the court were full of basic factual errors and I had to highlight corrections before sending them back *approved*. I checked back over my previous emails to see if I had omitted anything or had sent him the wrong information, but no, there it was in black and white, all present-and-correct. How could he be getting this wrong when I had provided everything he had requested, on time and in order? I phoned my lawyer's associate and politely mentioned that a number of key facts in the latest document were incorrect. I received no explanation or apology, just an assurance that they would correct the document. Hmm.

The court process was repetitive, with the same information required many times over. Mediation is an integral part of the family law process, and both parties must participate in mediation sessions in the hope that their matter can be resolved *before* the parties need to go to court. In my case this was just prolonging the suffering, as Artur had no intention of reaching any kind of financial settlement with me. Nevertheless, we had to go through the motions. He was often obstructive and evasive during our sessions and I was astonished that his lack of cooperation was tolerated.

By now I had grown disillusioned and dissatisfied with my legal representation. The bills were mounting and becoming more expensive, yet we seemed to be making no headway. It felt as though I was spinning my wheels. Wasn't this lawyer the best in town? I had a right to expect at least passable

SIXTEEN | Survival of the organised

representation, but the efforts to date had been definitely substandard.

I began looking for anything that would help me to improve this situation; perhaps I was at fault? Had I been missing something? Had I been getting in the way of the process? In desperation I started trawling through the Australian Family Law Court website to discover as much as I could about the Family Law process regarding financial orders, to see what I could do to be a more effective client.

I found an abundance of useful and relevant information that was written specifically for people like me going through the Family Law process. There were pages devoted to explaining the procedures, fact sheets, forms and guides to all aspects of Family Law. It was like going down a rabbit hole, each page or link lead to another avenue of useful information. I spent a great deal of time on that site and gleaned a better understanding of how the Family Law system worked and how cases were processed and determined.

I sat back and scratched my head and wondered if I could be more proactive in the *Application for Orders* process and contemplated that for a while. There were so many forms and how-to guides (which I read painstakingly) that I now had a clear understanding of what was required, the order in which it was required, and the process involved, that it struck me that the procedure was fairly straightforward. I had looked at the Family Law Court website when I had first engaged my lawyer, but I was looking at it then through an entirely different lens. Back then I reasoned that I would have a lawyer to represent me, so I didn't need to investigate the site too closely.

Another day brought another disappointing exchange with my legal team. Again, some of the basic and not-so-basic facts were incorrect, and this could have a detrimental bearing on the outcome of my application. I began to wonder if I would have more success by taking a leaf out of Artur's book and representing myself. I was paying significant amounts for below average service, and if this continued, I would soon be penniless and surely lose my case.

I pondered this problem and deliberated it for another week. I wasn't sure that I was capable of self-representation, yet it was evident that there were people taking this route, and that the Court allowed it. Fate intervened when I received yet another costly invoice from my lawyer. I wouldn't have objected if I

SIXTEEN | Survival of the organised

believed that progress was being made and that I was getting value for money. This made my decision for me, and I phoned the practice to explain that I would not be requiring their services any longer. They advised me that if I wanted my file, I would need to settle my account first. Fair enough. So, I scraped the not-inconsiderable amount together and paid the bill. A few days later I picked up my file from their office and felt a great sense of relief as soon as I walked out of the door. I guess I really should have been terrified by what I had just done but living with Artur had been just as scary most of the time, so this was no big deal. The bar had already been raised high on my fear-o-meter, so I was up for this new challenge.

Opening and reading through the file was empowering. I sat at the kitchen table and spread the contents out, sorting them into logical categories. I read each item carefully and made notes as I went, highlighting text and flagging pages where necessary. I have always processed information better when I have a visual representation of it, so I deployed my trusty method of filing everything into a ring binder (which eventually grew to several ring binders) by category. It meant that when I needed to access any information it was right at my fingertips. Over the next few days and weeks I read over my file many times, burning the contents into my brain until I knew my case like the back of my hand.

The first real test of my ability to represent myself came when I had to file a document with the Family Court. Until now my lawyer had done this for me, but this time I had to do it myself. I won't pretend that I wasn't intimidated by the prospect and I'm not too proud to admit that I felt physically ill the first time I walked into the Family Court building on my own. Sure, I had been in the building before now, but my lawyer had always accompanied me. Now it was just me, myself and I.

I nervously made my way through the foyer to enquire where I had to go to lodge my documents. The Court building was an imposing structure with a soaring atrium; everything was on such a vast scale that it was impossible not to feel small and vulnerable. No doubt it was obvious that I was a little lost and unexpectedly a court official stepped forward to speak to me. My initial thought was that he was going to tell me that I didn't belong there and that I should leave the building. Surprisingly he kindly asked if I needed help, and when I explained why I was there he walked me over to the registry desk so I could take a number and wait to be called. So far, so good.

SIXTEEN | Survival of the organised

Soon enough I was called over and I nervously handed over multiple copies of my documents with the official cover sheets completed ready for lodging. I felt like I was handing in a very important exam paper and watched while the registry attendant checked that everything was in order: all sections completed, correct file number quoted, attachments notated and secured correctly, all signed and dated. Somehow I passed the test, and once I had paid the filing fee my document was stamped accordingly. I was given a receipt acknowledging that it had been correctly filed before the due date and I was free to go.

I felt such relief at having this first big hurdle over with that I headed for the nearest café and had a quiet cup of tea to take time out to reflect on what I had just done. For those people engaged in the legal system it's an everyday occurrence, but for me it was a momentous occasion to lodge my first file in person at the Court. It wasn't overly difficult. Once I took my nerves out of the equation it was a straightforward process, not much more involved than doing a transaction in person at a bank. I could do this much at least, and it occurred to me that it wasn't necessarily survival of the fittest, it might just be survival of the organised!

These days most Court documents are submitted online, but the same principles still apply: you must have all your "i's dotted and t's crossed" before even thinking about uploading your files.

SIXTEEN | Survival of the organised

Learned Wisdom

- If you do engage a lawyer to represent you in any aspect of the Family Law system, be a proactive client. Ask what you can do to make their job easier to ensure you get the best possible representation
- However, if you are considering self-representation, make time to thoroughly explore the Family Law Australia website before making a decision. You need to be confident that you are capable of taking this route
- If you are not naturally organised, you will need to become organised. Self-representation is no place for the disorganised!

SEVENTEEN | So, how do I do this?

It had never been my intention to self-represent, as I held the belief that the professional was usually the best person for the job, and this instance was no exception. However, circumstances had conspired to push me in that direction and now I had to make the best of it. From a *glass half full* perspective, this new situation presented me with an unexpected opportunity to control how my case was managed. As I had given away any sense of control I had during my marriage, it was now a valued commodity. I presumed that I might be able to manage self-representation for the bulk of the legal process, and that as it got closer to the court hearing I would need to enlist professional help. And that's exactly what eventuated.

Buoyed as I was from my minor triumph in successfully filing my first documents with the Family Court, I knew that there would be many more documents to write and file, and it would be no easy road. It would require all my investigative, writing and organisational skills and perhaps a bit of help too.

THE GILDED CAGE

Let me be perfectly clear, I wouldn't recommend self-representation as a first choice of action; where possible, you should seek legal advice before deciding what is the best option for your matter. But if, for whatever reason, you elect to self-represent, let me share with you what I learned through experience. Or perhaps you are not self-representing but want to give your legal team everything they need to represent you in the best way possible. You can be a worthy assistant to your lawyer by promptly providing them with accurate and detailed information on request. This could save you valuable time and money.

My experience was solely regarding a financial settlement, but the protocols and methods I used could be applied if you are engaged in parenting and residency matters too. You can be an asset to your case, whatever it may be, if you understand the following principles.

Can I do this?

You may be surprised just how well-equipped you are to embark on a journey of self-representation, but as a bare minimum you will need to be moderately computer-literate; be able to construct grammatically correct sentences; have access

SEVENTEEN | So, how do I do this?

to the internet; and be self-disciplined enough to research, prepare, write and submit your documents according to the Court deadlines.

You will also participate in mediation sessions with your ex-partner, their legal team, and a magistrate or other court official. You need to be able to withstand these conferences, so perhaps take a support person if the court allows it.

Take the fear out of the equation

Don't be scared or overwhelmed by the task in front of you. Take a few deep breaths and take it one step at a time. If you have lived through domestic violence you will know how paralysing fear can be. Now is the time to let go of fear. Remember, the best way to eat an elephant is one spoonful at a time!

I did my best work when I was just a little bit angry, rather than at a time when I was upset or feeling vulnerable. While I don't recommend it as a lifestyle choice, keeping a little anger in reserve helped me to operate on adrenaline rather than despair, and fuelled many a late-night session at my keyboard. Equally, if you are feeling white-hot rage then it is also not the time for you to prepare any legal documents. Wait until you have calmed down sufficiently before you start writing, otherwise you will be creating emotion-fuelled work when what you need to be doing is *sticking to the facts*.

Commit time and space to the cause

Carve out some time in your calendar and commit to the process. If you have children, have someone mind them for you or wait until they are in bed, as distractions will not help you to think clearly. Turn off your phone, make yourself a cup of tea and clear enough space on your kitchen table to spread your documents out. Start by taking stock of your situation and write down in dot points what you know to be the relevant facts of your case.

Then think about what outcome you are seeking, what is it that you want to achieve? You need to have a clear picture about what you are hoping for so that you can effectively focus your time and energy.

Knowledge is power

Take plenty of time to explore the Family Court of Australia (or equivalent if you live in another country) website. It has a wealth of information to help you. Navigate your way around the pages, links and forms; bookmark them, save them, or print them off if it helps. Just about everything you will need to present your argument can be found there.

Create a folder system on your computer for your files and a matching physical folder system so you can have all information and documents to hand quickly.

I recall the first mediation session where I was representing myself. As my case files were bulky and heavy, I had no choice but to put them in a wheeled suitcase so I could transport them. I felt very self-conscious entering the room with my wheelie suitcase, and both Artur and the presiding magistrate exchanged looks as I took my seat. In the next instant it was down to business so there was no time to dwell on any embarrassment I may have felt. As the session progressed, the magistrate wanted to refer to a particular document and could not locate his copy amongst his materials. He asked if either Artur or I had a copy of it. Artur looked blank, he had few papers on the table in front of him and it suggested that he had prepared little for the meeting. Because I had my indexed folders with me, I was able to locate the document quickly for the magistrate. It was a document that related to a particular point I was attempting to make, and it was vital to the progress and outcome of that particular meeting. If I hadn't been able to produce it quickly, I would have been at a distinct disadvantage. It was an example of my 'survival of the organised' hypothesis proving to be likely.

Be in the 'write' frame of mind

Get into the right headspace before writing any material to make sure you are as calm and objective as you can be. It's worth repeating, so I will say it again: stick to the facts – ask yourself, what is relevant to this document or application or form? Your legal team (if you have one), court officials, the magistrate or the judge have limited time to consider your documents, so you need to include only what is relevant.

Not only is *what* you write important, so too is *how* you write. Make sure your words are typed legibly: consider 1.5-line spacing as a minimum; don't be tempted to use fancy typefaces as they can be difficult to read; check your formatting and ensure it is consistent across the entire document, and all your

SEVENTEEN | So, how do I do this?

documents for that matter. Dot points can be a useful tool in organising a lot of information in a way that is easy to process, and if you submit printed documents, print them single-sided only.

Give yourself plenty of time to research, prepare and write your documents, anything written in haste will be evident and it will not endear you to those who have to read it. Do a first draft, then a second draft, and then check it again, just to be sure that you really have been in the 'write' frame of mind. Have someone you trust proofread your work and make any edits or amendments before submitting them. You only get one shot at it, and it has to be your best work. Think of it like studying for a qualification: the more study, revision and prep work you do the better your exam results will be.

Enlist help where you can

My friend Sally was a veteran of the Family Law system, having separated and divorced some years before. She had gained a hard-won understanding of how the system operated during her numerous interactions regarding access and child support issues with her ex-husband.

So, Sally became my mentor or training buddy, and I used her as a sounding board when I was struggling with a task or how to frame a critical piece of information. It's worth having someone else to check your documents before finalising them, as it's easy to overlook minor mistakes or errors in your own writing.

Watch your language

Sally had given me some very useful advice when I was writing my first submission to the Court. She warned me against using any emotive language in my papers and to "'just stick to the facts". So, take care when writing your submissions. Emphatic statements will need to be qualified and worded carefully. For instance, a sentence such as "He/She hides money from me" might read better as "I believe that he/she has concealed income and assets from me because of [insert your reasons]". Equally, try rephrasing a statement such as "I know that he/she has a drinking problem" to "I am aware that my partner consumes a minimum of a bottle of wine every day". It is better to make specific factual observations rather than sweeping accusations.

Free or low-cost legal advice

If you are unable to afford legal representation, there are a number of avenues for you to access free legal advice. In Australia, the **Family Relationship Advice Line** offers free legal advice and information on services that may be able to help you. Their phone number is **1800 050 321**, or visit their website at *familyrelationships.gov.au*.

Free legal advice can also be obtained from any legal advice line or **Legal Aid** organisation in your state or territory. Visit *nationallegalaid.org* for contact details for legal aid services in your state or territory. It's worth noting that court staff are unable to give you legal advice.

The **Women's Legal Service Australia** operates in most states in Australia and provides free legal help for women with domestic violence and complex family law matters, among other services.

I used this service and found it to be **invaluable** in keeping me on track with my submissions. Their evening Drop-in Legal Advice Sessions were a godsend. I could speak directly with a female lawyer and I could seek clarification on any points of law or parts of the Family Law process that were unclear to me.

They would also check my final drafts before I submitted them to make sure they were fit to file. Free call the Australian Women's Legal Service on **1800 957 957** or visit their website at *wlsa.org.au.*

While I have cited the Australian sources for support services, there are corresponding ones in most Western countries, and they can usually be found by conducting a quick internet search. I strongly recommend that you enlist the help of free or low-cost legal services as they can be very helpful in guiding you from a legal perspective: are your documents compliant, do they address everything they need to, are they filed on time and in the correct manner?

Immerse yourself in the surroundings

It wasn't just the Family Court building itself that I familiarised myself with; at Sally's suggestion I sat-in quietly on some cases as they were being heard in court. She thought it would be beneficial for me to see how the proceedings unfolded in real time, and she was absolutely right. On a day and time when I knew that the Court would be in session, I approached the court usher. I explained that I would have a matter at a future date and asked if it would be possible for me to sit quietly at the rear

SEVENTEEN | So, how do I do this?

of the courtroom to observe the proceedings. Fortunately, the court usher gave me permission and so I gained a valuable insight into how a courtroom operates.

I learned that it is very procedural, and that the process and the Court must be respected. How you conduct yourself could influence how your matter is perceived. This is no time or place for point-scoring or poor behaviour. As I've said before, the Court just wants the facts, with no embellishment or dramatics. This was a valuable exercise that gave me a better understanding of the inner workings of the Court and what I could expect when my turn came.

Stand your ground

When you are facing up to a partner who has abused you, be prepared that they may try to intimidate you to discourage you from commencing or continuing your *Application for Orders*. Think in advance about what you will do, or say, when the inevitable happens.

I must have been making too much headway for Artur's comfort during one of our mediation sessions. When the magistrate was distracted while reading through some paperwork, Artur leaned across the table and said to me in a low voice, "I know where you live." He gave me his most menacing gaze and held it for longer than was necessary. I just ignored him and pretended that this news did not worry me, even though it was unsettling. I could not let him distract me as too much was at stake, so I pushed it to one side and stayed present in the moment.

Did Artur really know where I lived? He was a master tactician and I wouldn't have put it past him to lie about such a thing. He was trying to push all the right buttons to put me off my game and he knew this was a big one. I reasoned that even if he did know where I lived (which I doubted) Artur was on the local police radar, I lived in a secure complex and the onsite managers were vigilant. I would just tough this out and dial 000 if ever it came to it.

Not satisfied with this attempt to unnerve me, Artur tried again at the next mediation session. Normally after the sessions both parties politely avoided each other on their way out of the building. I had learned from my lawyer not to get into the same lift as the other party but to stay behind and wait for the next lift. This was the convention practised throughout the building.

SEVENTEEN | So, how do I do this?

This time, however, Artur ambushed me at the lift and dealt his ace card. He stepped in front of me to stop me from being able to enter the lift. Knowing he would only have a second or two before someone intervened, he threatened "Stop this case or I will take Tim away from you!" I looked him squarely in the eyes, stuck my chin out and said, "Knock yourself out trying!" I stepped around him, entered the lift and pressed the Close Door button. As the doors were closing, I steadily held his gaze. The look on his face said it all, he had not expected me to be so defiant and unperturbed by his childish threat. I had called his bluff. I knew he would never be capable of the energy and commitment required to care for a teenager. It was the last thing he would be inclined to do.

Nothing came of either of his idle threats, because that's all they were: petty and hollow attempts to stop me from proceeding with my application for a financial settlement.

Subpoenas and file viewings

As your case progresses you may need to request information or documents from the other party. This may be a request to your ex-partner or any associated person or entity relevant to your case. If a person refuses, or is unable of their own free will, to produce documents or give evidence at a hearing or trial, a party may request the Court to issue a subpoena directed to that person.

If the Court grants you permission to serve a subpoena, it is a fairly straightforward matter. As with most Family Court procedures, the subpoena form can be found on the Family Law Court website. It's a matter of reading through the form and following the accompanying instructions. Most likely you would not want to serve the subpoena yourself, as this needs to be done in person, so a process server can do this for you for a modest fee. Most of them will also file court documents for you for a small fee, if you don't have the time or the energy to do it yourself. I used a process server to serve subpoenas on the persons whom I believed had aided and abetted Artur to hide assets from the authorities, and as it turned out, from me too.

Once the other parties have provided information in compliance with your subpoena you may file a *Notice to Request to Inspect*. This is an application to the Court to inspect the supplied files or documents as requested on your subpoena. If the request is granted (and if you completed, filed and served your subpoena and application in accordance with the Court's

SEVENTEEN | So, how do I do this?

requirements your request should be granted), you will be able to arrange a time suitable with the court to view the documents. You will not be allowed to remove the documents from the Court, but you may take notes or make photocopies.

If you have safety concerns

Throughout your self-representation journey, it's likely that you will have a number of mediation sessions as part of the dispute resolution process. This means you will be in the same room as your ex-partner. If you have experienced domestic violence, particularly physical abuse, you may be concerned about having such close proximity to your abuser.

The courts place a priority on safety and can assist with the safety of you and your family when you are attending court. If you have any concerns for your safety, it is important you let the courts know well before your appearance is scheduled. The required notification time varies from state to state (it can be from five days up to 14 days) so you should check this information on the relevant website. If there is an existing family violence order it should be provided to the courts as soon as possible.

THE GILDED CAGE

Documentation, documentation, documentation

During one mediation session the Magistrate was specifically addressing the issue of the family home being placed in a third-party trust. He advised me that it would be very difficult to prove that Artur and I were the rightful owners of the property. At the end of the session he turned to me and said, "You have a long row to hoe, but I wish you luck." I could have given up there and then, but sometimes bloody-mindedness takes over good sense. I already knew it was going to be difficult to prove that the trust was a sham, a construct for Artur to conceal assets from me, creditors, the tax office, and anyone else who might have an interest in his financial affairs. It was precisely why I had secured, or made copies of, so many documents when I was preparing to leave Artur. Without documentary evidence I knew I would not have a leg to stand on. I had documents that suggested that we did own the house: building insurance policies on the property sent to our address and paid by us year after year; council rates notices sent to our address and paid by us; and evidence of maintenance and improvements made to the property in our name, also paid for by us. Either we were the real owners of the property or we were amazing tenants! I presented this proof as part of my *Evidence-in-Chief,* believing it

SEVENTEEN | So, how do I do this?

would surely be enough to make Artur's court-day legal team think twice, even if he did not.

I cannot stress enough how important it is to have documentary evidence to support your claims and arguments whatever they may be. Without supporting evidence, your chance of success will be slim.

It's a marathon not a sprint

You might be wondering how long it will take to navigate your way through the dispute resolution system until you reach an agreement between both parties and orders are handed down. Let me warn you that it is a marathon and not a sprint.

My matter appeared as pre-mediation and mediation sessions six times over an 18-month period before a court date was granted. It took nearly a year after separating to get to the first pre-mediation session, and it took three years from the day of separation to the point where the financial settlement was disbursed.

Imagine you are studying for a tertiary qualification; this should give you an appreciation of the commitment in energy and time required. You *can* dig deep to access your last ounce of determination and resilience to last the distance. If you have survived domestic violence you can probably survive fighting for what's fair. To illustrate my point, my *Evidence-in-Chief* (which is an affidavit stating all the circumstances of the case) was 28 pages long and had 52 annexures. The file in total was nearly four centimetres thick. Unless the judge agrees to it, once the applicant submits their *Evidence-in-Chief*, no further oral evidence is accepted. You can see how important it is to put in as much effort as you can to get your documents word-perfect.

EIGHTEEN | Judgement day

As I progressed through the dispute resolution process and a hearing date drew closer, it became evident that I would need to engage a lawyer once more, just to help me over the last hurdle. Again, Sally came to the rescue and mentioned a lawyer she had observed during her sessions in Court and whom she thought would be ideal. I contacted the recommended law practice and over the phone I explained that I had been self-representing up until now, but as a court date was drawing nearer, I knew that I needed some professional expertise on board. I met with the lawyer Sally suggested, and an associate of his, and the meeting could not have gone better.

They examined my files and commended me on my progress thus far. They were more than happy to represent me and to allow me to continue with preparing my *Evidence-in-Chief* and its lodgement. This meant I could save money on the tasks I was capable of, and only pay for the work I could not do. The associate and I worked closely together mostly, and only involved the partner when necessary, again reducing my expenses.

THE GILDED CAGE

When I first became aware that the associate lawyer would be my principal lawyer, I am ashamed to admit that I was a bit taken aback: she was just a slip of a girl and looked no more than eighteen years old. How wrong I was! I should have known, more than anyone, not to underestimate a determined woman. She proved to be a pocket rocket and a terrier all wrapped up in one perfect dynamic package. She was organised, knowledgeable, efficient and compassionate. She and I worked well in collaboration, and before too long we were ready to go to court.

A barrister was recommended, and I met with him twice prior to the court date to ensure that he had all the information he needed to argue (and hopefully win) my case. During my marriage I had observed Artur's tough take-no-prisoners negotiating style and I had learned to give as good as I got. In my application for financial orders, I sought the family home be signed over to me *in its entirety*. It was a bold move, but I knew I would get nowhere with Artur by playing nice. I had no illusion that I would be granted the entire family home, but I knew that he would try to beat me down, and if I started from a higher bargaining point I was more likely to get what I

EIGHTEEN | Judgement day

actually wanted, which was half the value of the family home. I figured that Tim and I were owed that much at the very least.

My day in court finally arrived. Sally offered to accompany me to court for the big day, and I was grateful to have her there. Having 'someone in my corner' took the edge off my nerves and gave me a like-minded soul to talk to during the lengthy periods when my barrister was elsewhere.

When we arrived, we were ushered into a small room which would remain our home room for the duration. The other party (Artur and his legal team) had a home room too, and the barristers negotiated together at some mysterious point in the middle. We knew that there was a strong possibility that we may not be granted a court room that day, meaning no **court** appearance, and that we would then be expected to settle out-of-court or wait until another sitting day became available. Cases regarding property issues (quite rightly) had a lower priority than cases regarding parenting issues, and as the daily register showed child dispute cases listed, we had a better than average chance of being bumped.

The system is designed to encourage parties to settle out of court. Given the cost of having your barrister present you are unlikely to hold out for yet another date just so you can have the privilege of standing in front of a judge. By the time you reach this stage of the proceedings you just want it over and done with. If they offered you a broom cupboard to settle in, you'd probably take it.

It was quickly confirmed that we had been unsuccessful in securing a courtroom and we would be proceeding to settle out-of-court. To the average person it's a curious thing to be part of, watching this strange dance between opposing sides. You needed to know the steps lest you should put a foot wrong. The barrister would leave our room and be gone for some time. Eventually he would return with a partial offer, which we would discuss in detail. We (the barrister and I) would either reject or accept part, or all, of the offer and he would again leave the room to relay the answer back to Artur's barrister.

Sometime later my barrister would return to us and we would wait for the other barrister to come back with an answer or counteroffer. If I'd been told we had to change ends at half time, I would have believed it!

This process was repeated many times, and it became a game of *who blinks first*. Finally, there was a breakthrough. My barrister

EIGHTEEN | Judgement day

returned with the latest offer from Artur. It was still at an insulting and unacceptable level and I was not tempted to agree to it. But then my barrister said something that was truly revealing; "They say the offer is only on the table for the next ten minutes". Years of observing Artur's bargaining and tough-guy negotiating style had served me well. 'The offer is only on the table for the next ten minutes' was straight out of his playbook.

I smiled as my barrister relayed this message to me. This was Artur trying to create a sense of urgency, or even panic, where none existed. I took a deep breath and replied, "Actually, I have all day, and there's no need to give an answer just yet". The barrister looked surprised by my response, but as far as I was concerned, I **did** have all day. As was required, I had already paid him in advance for a full day in court, so why not use it? I certainly wasn't going to get a refund for giving everyone an early mark. So, we waited, and waited, and rather than becoming nervous or agitated as the time slipped by, I became calmer and more confident.

Blink. You blinked; I saw you blink.

THE GILDED CAGE

It was well into the afternoon, when suddenly there was a flurry of activity. Whispered meetings in the corridor between the two barristers were becoming more frequent and more animated. I couldn't hear what was being said but I could read the body language anytime the door was left ajar and I sensed that something was brewing. Still, I remained calm and showed no acknowledgement of the activity outside the room. In the pre-smartphone world, there was nothing to distract us, so Sally and I chatted quietly about anything and everything to pass the time: our children, the weekend activities that were part and parcel of family life, what to cook for dinner that night. Anything to keep from focussing too much on what was at stake.

Finally, my barrister entered the room. There was confidence in his stride, and he looked more assured than he had at any other time that day. He had an eleventh-hour offer to present to me and it was no less than half the value of the family home. It seemed that my calculation in holding out and not being in a hurry to accept the first offer had paid off. I knew that all the players in this performance would be keen to get home. Did I mention that it was a Friday? Doesn't everyone want to start their weekend as early as possible? I signed on the dotted line,

EIGHTEEN | Judgement day

and after a few formalities, I was free to go home and free to start the next chapter in my new life

It's difficult to put into words how I felt having finally secured a settlement from Artur. It wasn't just about the money, although this amount would be enough for Tim and me to start over again, perhaps for a deposit on a home of our own. No, the sweetest victory had been in holding Artur to account. Making him take responsibility for the disgraceful way he had behaved as a father and a husband, and to face up to his deceit in hiding assets. The time had arrived for him to be taught a lesson and for life to stop rewarding his bad behaviour.

I presumed Artur would be incandescent with rage at having to part with one penny for the settlement. Remember, this was the man who was adamant that I deserved nothing, not a thing, and that regardless of any entitlement I might think I had, he had no assets anyway. I can only guess that his legal team had enough doubt about that for Artur to agree to settle out-of-court, and to award me my fair share of the family home.

I remember nothing about travelling home from Court, I had no plans to celebrate the extraordinary result to the day's proceedings. Even though I was on a high from the outcome, I was wrung-out, too. All the nervous energy I had been living on for weeks had been burnt up and there was nothing left in the tank. I fixed a light meal for me and Tim, had a shower, and fell asleep on the sofa while watching television in my pyjamas. The high-octane legal world was evidently not for me!

EIGHTEEN | Judgement day

Learned Wisdom

- You need to work *with* the legal system, not *against* it
- I had a disappointing experience with my first lawyer, but then I had an extremely positive experience with the next one. I just had to find a lawyer who was the right fit for me
- If I hadn't had that negative experience with my first lawyer, I would never have embarked on the empowering journey of self-representation
- Every cloud…

NINETEEN | The final act

The weeks that followed the out-of-court settlement were busy with the activity of placing the family home on the market and securing a successful sale. Bills needed to be paid and loose ends tied up, but none of these tasks were difficult or burdensome for me now. They represented the end result of a job well done.

In a bittersweet twist, I felt a strange kind of emptiness. The last three years had been consumed by the anxiety and the danger of the separation, the hard grind of starting over a whole new life, and the struggle of fighting for what I considered was justice. When the final account for my legal team was paid, I no longer had any contact with them, and I realised how much of a surrogate family they had become. I would talk to my pocket rocket lawyer no more, but surely that was the point, wasn't it? I was free finally from all the nonsense of dispute resolution, mediation and the legal process.

Did I feel cheated that I had been denied my day in court and did I think that being made to settle out-of-court was somehow a lesser victory? Not really. There had always been a real chance that we would not be granted a courtroom on our allotted day and that settling out-of-court would have been the only option, other than waiting for another date. And besides, even if we had waited for an alternative date, because our case was a financial matter and not a parenting matter, we still may not have been guaranteed a courtroom.

Nevertheless, a very dark part of me would have loved to have seen Artur on the stand and watch him squirm as he tried to justify why he placed the ownership of the house in a third-party trust, and to where the missing money from the businesses had been syphoned over the course of our marriage. But sometimes you just have to accept that things have a way of working out how they are meant to. It's conceivable that the courtroom process would have been more gruelling than settling out-of-court. And there was never a guarantee that the outcome would have been any more favourable, so the true costs might have outweighed the benefits anyway.

I never did find out where all the missing money from the businesses had disappeared to, because I couldn't afford to engage the services of a forensic accountant. Artur never paid one cent in child support for Tim, as he astonishingly had no

NINETEEN | The final act

money, even after selling the sweet shop. And I certainly never received a share of the funds from the sale of the sweet shop. Not a thing. But what I did come away with, and this was something that Artur could not take from me, was my freedom and my dignity. On the great balance sheet of life, I was wealthy beyond belief and I was happier than I had ever been.

In a perfect world, a part of me would love to have been granted full ownership of the house as recompense for all of Artur's deception and inexcusable behaviour that I had endured for 14 years. But here's the thing: you don't always get justice (or what you think justice should be) but you do get an outcome, and trust me, that is better than nothing.

Of course, if you don't accept the judgement or the outcome you are given you can always appeal, but I had had enough, and I wasn't going to start being greedy now. It was time to let go.

I relished my independence: I had been single now for three years (virtually for the first time in my adult life) and I wasn't going to give it up easily. Nothing could be as sweet as the autonomy I had earned through sweat and sacrifice. I now managed my life according to Tim's needs and my own. He was still my number one consideration, and I was not going to do anything that would upset the equilibrium I valued and cherished above all.

My social life consisted primarily of coffee catchups or taking in a movie with my friends, many of whom were part of my 'Ocean's 8', or mixing with the other parents at Tim's training sessions or sporting fixtures. Despite Maria's best efforts to match-make me with a series of 'eligible' bachelors, I resisted every attempt from her because I was truly happy to be on my own. It was more than enough for now. Never again did I intend to enter the Gilded Cage! (It would take a long time for me to learn to trust again and to enter into another relationship. It took a very special man indeed to win the heart of a much older and wiser me.)

I still had one more trip to make to the Family Court building, and that was to file my divorce papers. Now that the financial settlement had been finalised, it was time to be truly free of Artur, and that meant dissolving our marriage. Perhaps this should have saddened me, but I had already grieved for the loss of the relationship. Naturally, I completed my own paperwork for my divorce and filed it in person, as there was no online option at that time. After all the submissions I had made and

NINETEEN | The final act

filed, this was the easiest one of all. Once I had the *Decree Nisi* (a court order stating the date on which the marriage will end, unless a good reason not to grant a divorce is produced) all I had to do was wait for a month and a day and the *Decree Absolute* would be granted. It was the very last time I would walk out of the Family Court building, and as I did, I reflected on the anxious and insecure woman who had entered the building on her own for the very first time years earlier. She was no longer with me; instead she had been replaced with a much more confident and assured version. This new one was a much better form of the old me. I drove home from the Family Court building for the final time, and what did I listen to on my car stereo? Christina Aguilera's *'Fighter'*, of course.

TWENTY | Lessons learned

What did I learn during the long journey that took me from victim to survivor?

It was certainly a voyage of self-discovery, and it has taken me many years to reach the point where I could revisit the past and share my story with you. The process has sometimes been confronting as I have relived experiences I would rather forget. However, it will have been worthwhile if I can assure just one person that they can break the cycle of domestic abuse.

With the benefit of hindsight, I reflect on how my life has changed since the fateful day when I pushed the door of the Gilded Cage open. I marvel at how wide open the sky is and how far I can fly up into it. Never again will I allow my wings to be clipped; I will soar high into the air and I will refuse to be bullied or victimised. If I had my time over, I would care less about what people thought of me and I would air my dirty laundry if it meant exposing an abuser. I would know that being a nice girl could offer control over me on a plate to the wrong partner. I would understand that dignity and freedom are hard-won and priceless. And I would value them above all else.

Not for one second (with the exception of my panic on the first night out of the Gilded Cage!) have I regretted making a stand and taking back control of my life. I know now that it's absolutely okay to make mistakes, we are human after all. The tragedy is not in making the mistake in the first place; the tragedy is if you don't learn something from that mistake. My battle scars make me a far more interesting person than I might otherwise have been, and they help me to conduct myself with quiet dignity, knowing that whatever life throws at me I am able to withstand the worst. I can honestly say that I am thankful to Artur for placing me in circumstances that forced me to make a choice; I would not be the person I am today had I not endured all that I did.

While great progress has been made in recognising domestic violence and providing better services for those affected by it, there is still more work to be done. It will take generational change to educate our young men and women to be clear about what is acceptable behaviour and what isn't. As a society we need to remain vigilant, as there will always be those who think

TWENTY | Lessons learned

that it is their right to control and abuse others in the name of love.

My parting wish is that the awareness of domestic violence, in all its guises, will continue to be the subject of scrutiny, and that future generations will have the knowledge to recognise it, the courage to name it, and the resources to stop it. There *is* always hope, and you *can* break free from the cycle of abuse to create the life you deserve. It starts with a little self-belief and a giant leap of faith.

Acknowledgements

This book would not have been possible without the support, encouragement and guidance of the team at MJL Publications.

To Deborah Fay, who went above and beyond the role of Publisher in every instance to ensure that the dream became a reality. Your care, patience and expertise, given so freely, made the experience liberating and empowering.

To my remarkable editor at Snowflake Productions, who put the book through literary boot camp and whipped it in to beach-ready shape. "The impossible we do overnight; miracles take a little longer."

To Thomas Oliver for taking the photo for the front cover and capturing the spirit and message of the book in one glorious image.

To Ivan for coaching, guiding and encouraging me to finesse the final product. For your many, many hours of proof reading, and graphic design expertise so generously and kindly given. This book is all the better for your attention.

Thanks also to my fellow MJL Author Support Network buddies, particularly Rhonda Olsen, Di Riddell, and Romecca Sawyers, whose weekly video conference catchups kept me sane and energised when I had nothing left in the tank.

I will be eternally grateful to those officers of the Queensland Police Service who listened to me, believed me, and acted to ensure my safety, Tim's safety, and no doubt the safety of many others experiencing domestic violence, be it physical or non-physical abuse.

To my pocket rocket lawyer whose tenacity, professionalism, expertise and compassion restored my faith in the legal profession. Without you there would have been no justice, no outcome, no finish line.

To my beautiful son Tim, for your fearlessness in leaving the Gilded Cage with me, and for trusting me to navigate us both to a new and secure life. Giving me your blessing to share your story, so that others might benefit, is typical of your generosity and selflessness.

To my 'Ocean's 8' particularly, Eileen, Maria, Sally, Tina, Ian and Cathy, whose belief in me helped me to feel the fear and do it anyway. You will never know just how much of a difference your faith and generosity made in my life.

And finally, to my darling husband Andrew, whose love, encouragement, and inspiration has given me the freedom to believe that anything is possible. You are an example to all men, and there would be no book without your kindness to me, and all who have the privilege to know you.

www.ingramcontent.com/pod-product-compliance
Lightning Source LLC
Chambersburg PA
CBHW071658090426
42738CB00009B/1575